IN THE CITY OF GOLD

The Complete Burne Hogarth
Comic Strip Library

IN THE CITY OF GOLD

The Complete Burne Hogarth
Comic Strip Library

TITANBOOKS

TARZAN – IN THE CITY OF GOLD
The Complete Burne Hogarth Comic Strip Library

ISBN: 9781781163177

Published by Titan Books
A division of Titan Publishing Group Ltd.
144 Southwark St.
London
SE1 0UP

First Titan edition: April 2014

A CIP catalogue record for this title is available from the British Library

10 9 8 7 6 5 4 3 2 1

Printed in China

What did you think of this book? We love to hear from our readers. Please email us at: *readerfeedback@titanemail.com*, or write to us at the above address. To receive advance information, news, competitions, and exclusive offers online, please sign up for the Titan newsletter on our website: **www.titanbooks.com**

With thanks to George T. McWhorter, Ron de Laat, and Lisa Gordon Wither, to Peter Maresca and Bryce Hall for the remastering of the original strip, and to James Sullos, Cathy Wilbanks and Tyler Wilbanks of ERB, Inc.

CONTENTS

BURNE & BURROUGHS

THE STORY OF BURNE HOGARTH AND EDGAR RICE BURROUGHS

By Scott Tracy Griffin

Scott Tracy Griffin is the author of *Tarzan: The Centennial Celebration* (Titan Books, 2012). He has been researching and writing about Edgar Rice Burroughs for 25 years.

In 1936, Hal Foster, the artist responsible for the United Features Syndicate (UFS) classic *Tarzan* comic strips, advised his editors of plans to move to rival King Features Syndicate to concentrate on his medieval saga *Prince Valiant*. Foster developed *Valiant's* early pages at night, stockpiling pages for the launch while focusing on his *Tarzan* work by day. The artist, who officially resigned from UFS in December 1936, left a four-month backlog of strips to be printed. Aware that he was going to work for a competing syndicate, Foster sought to leave *Tarzan* on such an artistic high note that he would be impossible to replace.

He hadn't reckoned on 25-year-old Burne Hogarth.

Hogarth's compelling approach to art was suited to the era. At the height of the Great Depression, people, desperate to forget their respective struggles and dreaming of better days, devoured escapist fare delivered by movie palaces, radio programs, pulp magazines, newspaper comic strips, and comic books.

The '30s are often regarded as a high point in American pop culture, launching fictional heroes that continue to resonate today. Patrons flocked to see unforgettable films like *King Kong*, *The Wizard of Oz*, and *Gone with the Wind*. The Shadow, the Lone Ranger, and the Green Hornet enthralled radio listeners; Doc Savage and Conan the Barbarian captivated pulp magazine readers. Batman and Superman debuted in comic books, and the adventures of Flash Gordon and Dick Tracy were serialized in newspaper comic strips.

And across all media stalked author Edgar Rice Burroughs' immortal character Tarzan, an orphaned British aristocrat who attained heroic stature among the anthropoid apes of the African jungle.

Tarzan of the Apes, printed complete in the October 1912 issue of Munsey's pulp *All-Story*, captured its readers' imagination.

Burroughs, a mass-marketing genius, immediately complied with enthusiastic public demand by penning two dozen sequels; Tarzan was soon serialized in newspapers, onscreen in feature films and serials, on the Broadway stage, and on the radio. The ape man's image also endorsed products like ice cream, bread, and Signal gasoline with "The Power of Tarzan".

◇◇◇

As Burroughs penned *Tarzan of the Apes* in Chicago, Burne Hogarth was born across town on December 25, 1911. Max, Hogarth's father, was a carpenter and cabinetmaker; when young Burne tried to emulate his father's draftsmanship, he was encouraged to draw cartoons. The Hogarth family home was a gathering place of artists, which Burne later compared to a Parisian salon in shaping his formative creative development.

When Burne was 12, his father presented a sheaf of the boy's cartoons to the Art Institute of Chicago, which accepted the budding young artist for Saturday classes. By age 15, Hogarth was working professionally with the Associated Editors Syndicate, illustrating the series *Famous Churches of the World*. During this time, Hogarth worked a variety of odd jobs, including driving trucks, pressing laundry, and selling newspapers and shoes.

In 1929, he sold his first comic: *Ivy Hemmanhaw*, a single-panel gag strip, later creating *Odd Occupations and Strange Accidents* for Ledd Features Syndicate. Hogarth continued his education at Northwestern University and the University of Chicago, studying psychology and anatomy. His father's death in 1930 imbued an urgency into Hogarth's breadwinning efforts and furthered his resolve to succeed.

As the economic slump of the Great Depression deepened, Hogarth moved to New York, joining the Johnstone Agency and drawing comic advertisements. He also illustrated novelist Charles Driscoll's pirate strip *Pieces of Eight* for King Features Syndicate, and worked as an assistant at Fleischer Animation Studios, home to the Popeye and Betty Boop cartoons.

And, in 1937, when Hogarth presented some comic-strip ideas to UFS, editors countered with a request that he try out for Hal Foster's soon-to-be-available Tarzan strip.

The *Tarzan* newspaper strip was the brainchild of ad executive and Burroughs family friend Joseph Neebe. In 1927, Neebe traveled to Burroughs' Tarzana, California office to pitch the idea of a daily strip. Burroughs lobbied to hire his favorite illustrator, J. Allen St. John, but Neebe chose Hal Foster, then employed at Palenske-Young Advertising Art Agency in Chicago. R.W. Palmer of Campbell-Ewald scripted.

Neebe hoped to place the strip with William Randolph Hearst's King Features Syndicate, but Hearst's stipulation – that he retain film rights for Metro-Goldwyn-Mayer Studios where his paramour Marion Davies held a contract – wasn't possible. Universal, which held the option for ape man films, was readying the seventh Tarzan picture in a decade, the Frank Merrill serial *Tarzan the Mighty*.

Neebe eventually signed with Metropolitan Newspaper Syndicate, which merged with United Press Association later becoming part of the company's subsidiary, United Features Syndicate. *Tarzan of the Apes*, a ten-week daily strip (dubbed a picturization) of the novel by Foster, launched in thirteen U.S and two Canadian papers on January 7, 1929 – the same day the science fiction strip *Buck Rogers* premiered.

Initially disinterested in comic stripping, Foster returned to his advertising assignments, and Rex Maxon assumed artistic chores on the daily strip, which featured adaptations of Burroughs' novels. As the strip's popularity increased, Burroughs noted an uptick in sales of his novels.

The success of the daily strip warranted expansion; a color Sunday page, featuring original stories by Palmer and Maxon, debuted in 1931 in 37 newspapers. The juvenile storyline had Tarzan rescuing youngsters Bob and Mary Trevor from multiple threats, including an ape, a lion, cannibal pygmies, and pirates. Burroughs, dissatisfied and fearing this would typecast Tarzan as a children's tale, immediately pressed for a change in the creative direction.

The syndicate eventually capitulated to the author's wishes, re-hiring Hal Foster after 28 weeks. Maxon continued to illustrate the daily page novel adaptations. Though Foster's Sunday strips didn't follow the novels (largely omitting Tarzan's family and supporting characters), Burroughs' spirit was there, embodying Tarzan with an epic, heroic presence that discovered lost civilizations and raced across the length and breadth of Africa.

As Foster's full-page Sunday strips enchanted readers, Tarzan's popularity continued to grow. M-G-M, Hollywood's pre-eminent studio, optioned the property for a series of six hit films starring Johnny Weissmuller and Maureen O'Sullivan as the ape man and his mate Jane. Tarzan was also now broadcast into homes via a popular radio serial starring Jim Pierce, a former silent screen Tarzan, and his wife Joan (Burroughs' daughter).

Despite the burgeoning success of the Tarzan character and the acclaim that came with the artistic association, Foster elected to move on – and Burne Hogarth's position as one of the ape man's most admired illustrators commenced.

◇◇◇

Hogarth won the UFS assignment on the strength of his sample pages, in which he attempted to emulate Foster's style for a seamless transition. Hogarth segued into his own style as the strip's renown grew; he often spent five or six days drawing one page. Like Foster, he eschewed models, preferring to rely on his own creativity.

Hogarth's first published page, #322, appeared on May 9, 1937, continuing Foster's 70-week story "Tarzan in the City of Gold". As in Foster's tenure, each page culminated in a cliffhanger, ending with the next installment's title to tantalize readers in the manner of a weekly film serial.

Burroughs, steeped in the classics of Latin and Greek, had imbued Tarzan with a mythical stature, which Hogarth's formidable skill realized perfectly. A daydreamer who had witnessed the taming of the Western frontier firsthand, Burroughs had also, consciously or not, crafted a perfect escapist hero for the Industrial Age.

Danger is everywhere in Hogarth's *Tarzan* strip, in jagged, spiky leaves, branches, rocks, horns, claws, teeth, and other threats. His Tarzan's face reflects fury, resolve, shock, and every other emotion, heightened by his posture and motion. Hogarth's influences, which included classical Greek sculpture, Michelangelo and the Baroque

artists, German expressionism, Oriental art, and modern cinema, are evident in his composition.

In 1943, many newspapers reduced their full-page adventure strips to one-half page, crowding more strips onto Sunday sections reduced from sixteen pages to eight or ten, due to wartime rationing of resources and a desire to wring the most advertising and subscription money from the papers' popular attractions. Hogarth was unhappy with this change, and continued to produce full pages for holdout newspapers; a variant, horizontal version of his strip, with an extra "throwaway" panel was also produced for the half-pages, but Hogarth's art suffered from the reduction in size and clarity. That year, scripter Don Garden left to serve with the OSS in the war effort and Hogarth began writing his own material.

When Hogarth discovered his work was being reprinted in European books without additional royalty payments, he asked UFS to adjust his compensation. Unhappy with the syndicate's offer, he resigned. His final strip, #768 appeared on November 25, 1945, during the "Tarzan against Orizu-Khan" sequence. Puerto Rican artist Reuben Moriera assumed artistic duties under the pen name "Rubimor"; he had been recruited from his post on the Fiction House *Jungle Stories* comics featuring Ka'anga, an imitation Tarzan.

Hogarth created the Sunday strip *Drago*, featuring a young Argentine gaucho combatting Nazis in postwar Latin America, for the New York Post Syndicate. The strip never caught on with the public, and was serialized in few newspapers, running from November 4, 1945 to November 10, 1946. The following year, Hogarth and his friend Silas H. Rhodes, a war veteran and educator, founded the

ABOVE LEFT TO RIGHT The evolution of the Tarzan strip through Hogarth's first tenure from Hal Foster (left), through Hogarth (middle) to Reuben Moreira [Rubimor] (right), highlights the distinct styles of each era.

RIGHT Burne Hogarth's final Tarzan strip from August 1950, with his trademark spiky foliage and dynamic action scenes.

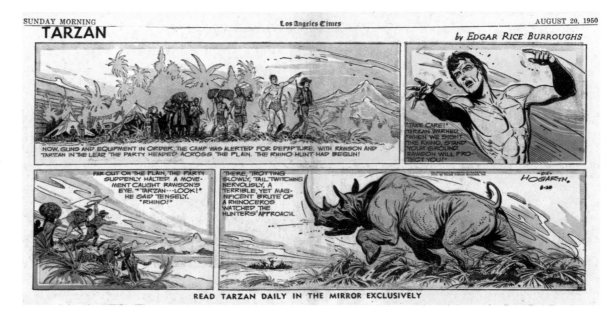

Cartoonists and Illustrators School to provide returning soldiers with an education and employable trade. In 1955, they changed the name to the School of Visual Arts (SVA) in New York City, where it still flourishes.

Rubimor's contribution to *Tarzan* proved short-lived, and the syndicate released him after 88 weeks. Hogarth accepted a raise and returned to the strip with #857, on August 10, 1947, finishing Rubimor's "Tarzan and the Island of Ka-Gor" storyline; he was also tasked with overseeing the daily strip; that illustration was farmed out to Dan Barry, though Hogarth's name appeared on the strip. Throughout the rest of Hogarth's tenure, daily strip artists, including John Lehti, Paul Reinman, and Nick Cardy, were hired by Hogarth and dubbed as "assistants" by the syndicate, which sought to capitalize on his name and achieve a continuity of styles between the two strips, although the storylines remained separate.

At Burroughs' behest, scripter Rob Thompson, who had worked for the author on the Tarzan radio program, two Decca Record albums, and the Dell Four-Color *Tarzan* comics, was hired in 1947 to write the newspaper strip continuity, supervised (and occasionally rewritten) by Burroughs. On May 12, 1950, following Burroughs' March 19 death, UFS released Rob Thompson from his writing duties. Hogarth penned one daily story, "Tarzan and Hard-Luck Harrigan," a light comedy, before UFS hired Dick Van Buren to script.

Hogarth left the Tarzan strip for good on August 23, 1950, #1015, with "Tarzan and the Wild Game Hunter" concluded in four weeks by Bob Lubbers, who also inherited the daily strip. Hogarth drew a total of 597 Sunday pages during his two stints.

Hogarth devoted himself to the SVA, and wrote art instruction books, including *Dynamic Anatomy* (1958), *Drawing the Human Head* (1965), *Dynamic Figure Drawing* (1970), *Drawing Dynamic Hands* (1977), *Dynamic Light and Shade* (1981), and *Dynamic Wrinkles and Drapery* (1992).

Two decades after leaving Tarzan, Hogarth returned to the character in triumphant fashion, illustrating the graphic novels *Tarzan of the Apes* (1972) and *Jungle Tales of Tarzan* (1976), his favorite of Burroughs' Tarzan books.

Hogarth's work was appreciated overseas even more than in the U.S.; his work was exhibited in one-man shows worldwide, including at the Louvre in Paris and the Museu de Arte in São Paulo, Brazil. French critics dubbed him "The Michelangelo of the Comics." In the 1980s, he moved to Los Angeles, where he taught at the Otis School and the Art Center of Pasadena, and served as a guest lecturer at schools like SVA and Parsons School of Design.

Hogarth passed away on Sunday, January 28, 1996, age 84, in Paris, France, following his appearance at the International Comics Festival in Angoulême, the world's largest comic art convention. He was survived by sons Michael, Richard, and Ross, and his former wife, Connie.

Of UFS's designation of him as Foster's successor, Hogarth later noted, "I was bowled over by this . . . because Foster was really a god of the comics." It's fair to say that Burne Hogarth, whose work continues to gain admirers and influence later generations, also stands with the giants in the world of illustration.

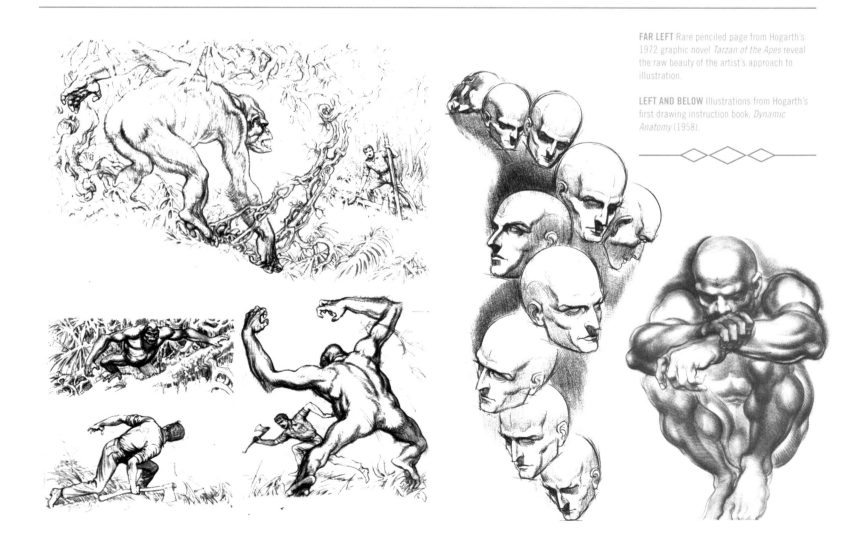

FAR LEFT Rare penciled page from Hogarth's 1972 graphic novel *Tarzan of the Apes* reveal the raw beauty of the artist's approach to illustration.

LEFT AND BELOW Illustrations from Hogarth's first drawing instruction book, *Dynamic Anatomy* (1958).

HAL FOSTER'S TARZAN IN THE CITY OF GOLD

SHE RELATED THE MISTY LEGEND OF HER ANCESTORS, WHO HAD FLED FROM WAR-TORN ASIA MINOR TO FOUND A KINGDOM HERE.

Tarzan in the City of Gold was begun with strip number 271 on May 17, 1936, by writer Don Garden and illustrator Hal Foster. When Foster left after 51 weeks, to focus his attention on *Prince Valiant*, United Feature Syndicate brought Burne Hogarth on board to complete the story. His first installment appeared on Sunday, May 9, 1937, with strip #322...

The story so far

The hidden kingdom of Taanor was settled by a group of refugees who sailed, long ago, to escape strife in war-torn Asia Minor. Landing in Africa, they built the walled city of Balakan, creating a haven for many of the region's indigenous tribes who came to dwell under their peaceful rule.

In Taanor they discovered gold so plentiful that to them its only value lay in coloring the domes and towers of the city. Generations passed, and Balakan came under the rule of the benevolent King Dalkon and his daughter, Princess Nakonia.

Adventurers Jim Gorrey and Rufus Flint learned of the vast treasure and organized a mercenary force, setting out across Africa. In the jungle, Gorrey stumbled upon a procession carrying the princess, just as a rogue rhinoceros attacked, killing Nakonia's guardian lion and charging her palanquin. Gorrey stepped in and shot the horned beast. He was hailed as a hero and the grateful princess invited him to join her group.

Hot in pursuit, Tarzan was traveling with Flint. But when they came within sight of the royal procession—just outside of the city walls—Gorrey convinced Nakonia that these were his enemies. She immediately dispatched the six lions that guarded the gates of the City of Gold, issuing an order: "Kill."

When Tarzan dispatched the foremost beast, the princess feared for the safety of the rest, and ordered them to withdraw. The Ape-Man was declared a foe of the golden realm, and he and Flint fled.

Later Tarzan infiltrated the city, learning of a plan to kill the king. He foiled the plot, but was captured and condemned to die at the hands of Lethor, a killer lion. However, he tamed the lion and

escaped. When Tarzan was recaptured, the king declared, "He has been officially executed. In the eyes of the law he is dead." Thus he was freed, and began to attract a group of followers.

As Nakonia's rescuer, Gorrey declared his intent to marry the princess. He and his cohort tricked the king into signing a document that made Flint the Prime Minister—the virtual dictator of Balakan. Flint tried to shoot Tarzan, but instead wounded the princess, and the Ape-Man fled into the forest with her.

Both in the forest and the city, Tarzan and his rebels harassed the forces under Flint's control. But the ranks of the mercenaries swelled, and the rebels were captured—forced to work in the gold mines. Escaping their captors, they cut off Flint's contact with the outside world. Yet the mercenary got word to his allies, and armed airplanes appeared in the sky.

The tyrant devoted himself to extending his empire of evil, and tribe after tribe was brought under his iron rule. In a daring move, Tarzan hijacked a plane, parachuted into the enemy camp, and destroyed all but one of the aircraft. Flying over the city, he dropped a message scrawled in his own blood.

Your vultures are no more.

TARZAN IS EAGLE OF THE SKIES.

The people rose up against the dictator. From hundreds of lips burst the battle-cry: "For King, for country, and for Freedom!" King Dalkon was brought forth, and Flint threatened to execute him. But Dalkon killed himself—with his last breath he cried, "Fight on! Follow Tarzan!" The Ape-Man captured Gorrey and Flint, and in a moment of mercy, allowed them to escape.

SOON THE CORTEGE EMERGED ONTO A PLAIN, IN WHICH LAY THE MYSTERY CITY OF BALAKAN, CAPITAL OF THE GOLDEN REALM.

GORREY'S GREEDY HEART EXULTED WHEN HE BEHELD THE GLITTERING DOMES AND SPIRES OF GOLD.

TARZAN, THOUGH HE BELIEVED DEATH CERTAIN, RESOLVED TO FIGHT TO THE LAST. HE CHARGED THE NEAREST BEAST.

SKILFULLY HIS KNIFE DID ITS ACCUSTOMED WORK, BUT THE REMAINING BRUTES CLOSED IN WITH FRESH FURY.

"The tyrant has fled," he proclaimed to the people. "Victory is ours!" Princess Nakonia returned and was crowned Queen, naming Tarzan as her War Chief. But as peace descended on the City of Gold, Gorrey and Flint met with Rakka, an international conspirator, and began to raise an army—one which would hurl its powerful engines of modern warfare against the Ape-Man's primitive forces.

Learning of their plans, he plunged into the jungle to spy on the army and harass them from the trees. As he did so, Flint's planes attacked Balakan, dropping bombs filled with poison gas. He delivered an ultimatum, so that when Tarzan returned he found Nakonia raising the flag of surrender.

"The War Chief of Taanor refuses to surrender," he declared.

"You are no longer my War Chief," she replied, despite her love for him. "You are under arrest. Guardsmen, seize him."

AT DAWN THEY HEARD THE SWIFT PURSUERS. TARZAN HID NAKONIA IN A TREE, LEFT LETHOR ON GUARD, AND MARSHALED HIS SWORDSMEN

Tarzan

by EDGAR RICE BURROUGHS

A LONG CHANCE

SADLY THE QUEEN ORDERED TARZAN'S ARREST. SHE KNEW NO OTHER WAY TO RESTRAIN HIS FIGHTING SPIRIT.

THE APE-MAN FROWNED. "WE DROVE OUT THE TYRANT BY THE SWORD. NOW YOU WOULD LET HIM RETURN WITHOUT A STRUGGLE."

"WHAT GOOD ARE SWORDS," NAKONIA SIGHED, "AGAINST THE ROARING BIRDS OF DEATH?"

"TARZAN WILL DESTROY THEM," HE REPLIED. "TARZAN IS MIGHTY," SHE SMILED; "BUT HE CANNOT REACH INTO THE SKIES."

"TARZAN WILL DESTROY THEM," HE REPEATED; AND THE QUEEN WAS PERSUADED. "YOU MAY TRY," SHE NODDED.

THUS FREED, THE RESOURCEFUL APE-MAN LAUNCHED A SERIES OF MYSTIFYING ACTIVITIES.

FROM THE WEAVERS AND ROPEMAKERS HE COLLECTED THEIR FINEST WARES.

INTO THE FOREST HE DISPATCHED A GREAT PARTY TO GATHER THE GUM OF A CERTAIN TREE.

AND ALL THESE MATERIALS WERE BORNE OUTSIDE THE WALLS WHERE WORKERS OF MANY CRAFTS WERE ASSEMBLING.

FROM GROUP TO GROUP TARZAN HURRIED GIVING HASTY BUT ACCURATE INSTRUCTIONS.

THE WORKERS BELIEVED HE WAS MAD. WHAT DID ALL THIS HAVE TO DO WITH TRAPPING THE DEVIL BIRDS?

HOGARTH

AND TARZAN HIMSELF WONDERED IF HIS FANTASTIC SCHEME WOULD SUCCEED AGAINST FLINT'S AIRFLEET.

NEXT WEEK: **THE WEB OF DEATH**

Tarzan
by EDGAR RICE BURROUGHS

WEB OF DEATH

DAY AND NIGHT THE ARTISANS LABORED UNDER TARZAN'S MYSTERIOUS INSTRUCTIONS; AND ON THE THIRD DAY----

----SEVERAL GIANT ENVELOPES OF LIGHT FABRIC WERE COMPLETED, AND PAINTED WITH THE ELASTIC TREE-GUM VARNISH.

AT THE MOUTH OF EACH A FIRE WAS BUILT, FOR THESE WERE SIMPLE BALLOONS, INFLATED BY HOT AIR.

THE RESOURCEFUL TARZAN WAS APPLYING THE FAMILIAR PRINCIPLE THAT HEATED AIR IS LIGHT, AND THEREFORE RISES.

AND NOW, TO THESE BALLOONS WERE ATTACHED GREAT NETS OF LATTICED ROPE.

NIGHT FELL, AND FLINT'S AIRFLEET ROARED ACROSS THE STARLIT HORIZON, SHADOWY MESSENGERS OF DEATH.

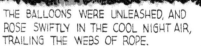

THE BALLOONS WERE UNLEASHED, AND ROSE SWIFTLY IN THE COOL NIGHT AIR, TRAILING THE WEBS OF ROPE.

THE PILOTS ZOOMED ON, THINKING ONLY OF THE HAVOC THEY WOULD WREAK ON THE DARKENED, DEFENSELESS CITY.

SUDDENLY THEY PERCEIVED THE ROPE MESH— TOO LATE. THE PLANES STRUCK!

PROPELLERS WERE FOULED, WINGS WERE ENTANGLED, THE PILOTS LOST CONTROL, AND THEIR SHIPS TUMBLED EARTHWARD.

AMID SHOUTS OF JOY THE "DEVIL-BIRDS" CRASHED AND BURST INTO FLAMES.

BUT NO VICTORY CRY LEFT TARZAN'S LIPS. HE KNEW THE REAL FIGHT WITH FLINT WAS STILL TO COME!

HOGARTH.

Next Week :- Elephants of Steel

Tarzan

by EDGAR RICE BURROUGHS

ELEPHANTS OF STEEL

WHEN TARZAN'S INGENIOUS TRAP HAD BROUGHT DOWN THE ENEMY AIRFLEET, HE WAS HAILED AS A MIGHTY HERO.

NOW THE PEOPLE WERE INFUSED WITH NEW SPIRIT. "NO SURRENDER!" THEY CRIED; "WE'LL FIGHT TO THE END!"

AND SEEING THE TEMPER OF HER SUBJECTS THE QUEEN RESTORED TARZAN TO HIS RANK AS WAR CHIEF OF TAANOR.

QUICKLY HE ORGANIZED AN ASSAULT BATTALION FOR SWIFT THRUSTS AGAINST FLINT'S FORCES.

FROM A FOREST AMBUSH, THE MEN OF TAANOR RAINED DEADLY ARROWS ON THE INVADERS.

BUT FLINT'S TRAINED INFANTRY RALLIED QUICKLY. RIFLES CRACKED; AND MANY OF TARZAN'S BRAVEST DIED.

NEXT DAY THE MECHANIZED COLUMN MOVED EASILY ACROSS A PLAIN GROWN TALL WITH GRASS.

SUDDENLY TARZAN'S MEN ROSE UP FROM HIDING, AND AGAIN A DELUGE OF MISSILES ASSAILED THE MERCENARIES.

THEN THE TANK CAPTAIN SHOUTED A COMMAND. THE RATTLING MONSTERS WHEELED, AND ROARED ACROSS THE PLAIN.

TARZAN'S COHORTS FLED IN TERROR BEFORE THESE STAMPEDING "ELEPHANTS WITH HIDES OF STEEL."

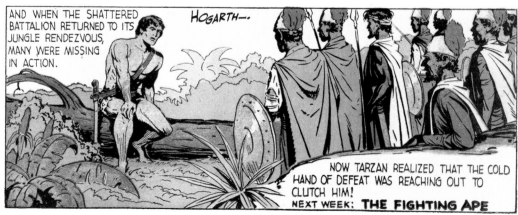

AND WHEN THE SHATTERED BATTALION RETURNED TO ITS JUNGLE RENDEZVOUS, MANY WERE MISSING IN ACTION.

HOGARTH—.

NOW TARZAN REALIZED THAT THE COLD HAND OF DEFEAT WAS REACHING OUT TO CLUTCH HIM! NEXT WEEK: THE FIGHTING APE

Tarzan

by EDGAR RICE BURROUGHS

© 1937, Edgar Rice Burroughs, Inc.—Tm. Reg. U.S. Pat. Off.
Produced by Famous Books and Plays. Distributed by
UNITED FEATURE SYNDICATE, Inc.

325—5-30

THE FIGHTING APE

THE INVADING COLUMN PUSHED STEADILY, RELENTLESSLY TOWARD THE GOLDEN CITY.

SAFELY QUARTERED IN HIS ARMORED CAR, FLINT CHUCKLED: "WHAT CAN THESE SAVAGES DO AGAINST SCIENCE?"

TARZAN WAS OCCUPIED BY THE SAME THOUGHT AS HE SURVEYED THE BULLET-THINNED RANKS OF HIS BATTALION.

IT WAS FUTILE INDEED TO OPPOSE TANKS, MACHINE GUNS, AND RIFLES WITH BRITTLE SPEARS AND ARROWS.

SUDDENLY THE SKIES FILLED WITH CLOUDS AND A LIGHT RAIN FELL. THE TAANORIANS CRIED OUT HAPPILY.

"SOON WILL COME THE BIG RAINS. OUR FOE WILL BE STUCK FAST IN THE MUD. ONLY TARZAN CAN TRAVEL THEN."

AN IDEA FLASHED INTO THE APE-MAN'S MIND. HE GAVE HURRIED INSTRUCTIONS, AND SWUNG INTO THE TREES.

HE WOULD ORGANIZE THE CHAOTIC NATURAL FORCES OF THE JUNGLE FOR A STUPENDOUS CAMPAIGN AGAINST THE INVADERS!

BUT SOON HE CLASHED WITH ONE OF THE VERY FORCES WHOSE AID HE SOUGHT—A FIERCE BELLIGERENT APE!

"KREEGAH!" TARZAN CRIED. THE MASSIVE ANTHROPOID GAVE NO HEED TO HIS WARNING.

"I KILL!" THE GREAT BEAST GROWLED, AND HURLED HIMSELF AT THE MAN-THING. AND FROM THE MOUNTAINSIDE THE WHOLE APE TRIBE POURED DOWN TO ENGULF THE STRANGER!
NEXT WEEK: **TARZAN BALKED**

HOGARTH

Tarzan
by Edgar Rice Burroughs

© 1937 Edgar Rice Burroughs Inc.—Tm. Reg. U.S. Pat. Off.
Produced by Famous Books and Plays. Distributed by
UNITED FEATURE SYNDICATE, Inc.

TARZAN BALKED

AS THE APE LUNGED, TARZAN DODGED, THEN LEAPED AND LOCKED AN ARM AROUND THAT HAIRY NECK.

"KAGODA!" THE BEAST GASPED, BUT HIS SURRENDER LEFT TARZAN STILL TO FACE THE ON-RUSHING TRIBE.

SUDDENLY FROM THE RACING HORDE BURST A HOARSE CRY: "MAN-THING IS TARZAN. DO NOT HARM HIM!"

TARZAN RECOGNIZED THE VOICE OF BOHGDU, HIS APE FRIEND WHO HAD SHARED WITH HIM SO MANY PERILOUS ADVENTURES!

IN APE FASHION, BOHGDU GREETED HIM BY EXAMINING HIS SKIN, THUS TO JUDGE HIS HEALTH.

THEN TARZAN ASKED: "WHO IS KING AMONG YOU?" BOHGDU BEAT HIS CHEST PROUDLY.

"BOHGDU MET THIS TRIBE: KING CHALLENGED BOHGDU. BOHGDU KILLED KING: NOW BOHGDU KING!"

BUT TARZAN SAW THAT THE BULLS RESENTED THE ALIEN MONARCH WHO RULED BY RIGHT OF CONQUEST.

THE JUNGLE LORD SAID: "MEN WITH THUNDER-STICKS INVADE OUR FOREST. TARZAN NEEDS AID."

"BOHGDU'S BULLS FIGHT BY TARZAN'S SIDE; KILL TARZAN'S ENEMIES!" THE KING ANNOUNCED.

THE BULLS GROWLED. "LET TARZAN FIGHT OWN BATTLES. WE NOT FIGHT, WE NOT DIE FOR HIM!"

THE APE-MAN TURNED AWAY. HE HAD FAILED IN HIS FIRST ATTEMPT TO RECRUIT A JUNGLE ARMY AGAINST HIS FOES!

NEXT WEEK: **GOOD FOR EVIL**

Tarzan

by Edgar Rice Burroughs

GOOD FOR EVIL

WHEN THE BULL APES REFUSED TO JOIN HIS JUNGLE ARMY, TARZAN TURNED AWAY.

BUT BOHGDU THE KING, WHO WAS TARZAN'S FRIEND, SNARLED ANGRILY AT HIS STUBBORN SUBJECTS.

"IF YOU NOT FIGHT FOR TARZAN, BOHGDU KILL!" HE THREATENED.

BUT THE JUNGLE LORD STAYED HIM. "TARZAN WANTS ONLY FIGHTERS WITH WILLING HEARTS."

TARZAN TURNED AWAY AGAIN AND THE KING FOLLOWED HIM, SAYING: "BOHGDU LEAVE THIS TRIBE, FIGHT FOR TARZAN!"

THE BULLS GRUNTED APPROVAL OF THE STRANGE ABDICATION, THEN FELL TO FIGHTING FOR THE ABANDONED KINGSHIP.

BUT SUDDENLY FROM THE PLATEAU ABOVE CAME PIERCING SHRIEKS, MINGLED WITH THE ROAR OF MARAUDING BEASTS.

TARZAN UNDERSTOOD THOSE AWFUL SOUNDS. PROWLING LIONS HAD DISCOVERED THE UNPROTECTED SHES AND THEIR TINY BALUS.

THE BULLS CEASED THEIR FIGHTING AND STOOD FOR A MOMENT BEWILDERED.

THEN THEY SCURRIED UP THE MOUNTAIN SIDE TO DO BATTLE AGAINST THEIR JUNGLE ENEMIES.

LEADING THEM ALL WAS TARZAN, TO WHOM THEY HAD REFUSED THE AID HE ASKED.

HOGARTH

AND WHEN HE REACHED THE PLATEAU HE SAW TWO HUGE LIONS CHARGING A PITIFUL TRIO OF BABY APES.

NEXT WEEK: CONFLICT

Tarzan in the City of Gold   17

Tarzan

by Edgar Rice Burroughs

CONFLICT

AS TARZAN SAW THE LION AND LIONESS DASHING AT THE TERRIFIED BALUS, HE SHOUTED: "LETHOR! HALT!" THE TAWNY-MANED BEAST STOPPED SHORT, FOR THIS WAS THE LION TARZAN HAD TRAINED TO DO HIS BIDDING.

BUT TARZAN MEANT NOTHING TO THE LIONESS, WHICH WAS LETHOR'S NEW-FOUND MATE. SHE CONTINUED HER FIERCE CHARGE.

THE APE-MAN HURLED HIMSELF THROUGH THE AIR AND ALIGHTED ON HER BACK.

AS THE IMPACT STRUCK THE BEAST TO THE GROUND, HIS POWERFUL ARMS LOCKED AROUND HER NECK.

FLYING TALONS, SNAPPING FANGS, AND THE LIGHTNING MOVEMENTS OF THE MAN MINGLED IN A DAZZLING WHIRL.

RISKING HIS LIFE, TARZAN FOUGHT BARE-HANDED; FOR HE WISHED ONLY TO SUBDUE, NOT TO KILL, LETHOR'S MATE.

MEANWHILE, BOHGDU BORE THE BALUS INTO THE TREES, WHENCE THE APE-TRIBE WATCHED THE FRIGHTFUL CONFLICT.

THERE WAS ANOTHER WATCHER, TOO--LETHOR, THE LION, QUIVERING WITH EXCITEMENT.

UNCONSCIOUSLY, HE WAS TORN BETWEEN HIS DOG-LIKE DEVOTION TO TARZAN AND THE IMPULSE TO HELP HIS MATE.

SUDDENLY THE LIONESS ROARED IN PAIN. THAT ROAR WAS A FIERY SPARK; LETHOR'S WILD INSTINCTS EXPLODED!

HOGARTH

HE CHARGED DOWN UPON THE STRUGGLING PAIR--TO GIVE AID TO HIS HAPLESS MATE!

NEXT WEEK: *THE BLOOD OF TARZAN*

Tarzan
by Edgar Rice Burroughs
THE BLOOD OF TARZAN

329-6-27

DRIVEN BY HIS WILD, NATURAL INSTINCTS, LETHOR RUSHED TO JOIN THE FRAY IN BEHALF OF HIS MATE.

THEN THE EXCITED BOHGDU SWUNG DOWN TO GIVE AID TO THE APE-MAN, WHO WAS HIS FRIEND.

TARZAN STRUGGLING WITH THE LIONESS SAW LETHOR'S MAD CHARGE. "LETHOR, HALT!" HE SHOUTED.

THAT COMMANDING MAGNETIC VOICE ELECTRIFIED LETHOR'S MEMORY OF TARZAN'S TRAINING. AUTOMATICALLY, HE STOPPED. IN HIS OBEDIENCE THERE WAS A MEASURE OF FEAR, FOR HE, TOO, HAD BEEN CONQUERED BY TARZAN.

BEFORE HIS INSTINCTS COULD GAIN SWAY AGAIN, TARZAN CALLED TO HIM GENTLY.

THE WORDS MEANT NOTHING TO HIM, BUT HE WAS SOOTHED AND REASSURED BY TARZAN'S TONE.

BOHGDU, HOWEVER, FELT THAT THE LION HAD PAUSED MERELY TO AWAIT A BETTER OPENING.

THE APE ADVANCED. LETHOR WHIRLED. THEN THESE TWO—BOTH TARZAN'S ALLIES!—CLASHED IN FRENZIED COMBAT.

MEANWHILE, TARZAN WAS HARD-PRESSED FOR THE LIONESS TWISTED HER HEAD AND SANK HER FANGS INTO HIS FLESH!

THE JUNGLE LORD'S STEEL GRIP FORCED HER TO RELEASE HER JAWS.

BUT NOW THE BEAST WAS INFLAMED TO NEW FIGHTING FURY. SHE HAD TASTED BLOOD!

HOGARTH—

NEXT WEEK: *SOLDIERS OF THE JUNGLE*

Tarzan

by EDGAR RICE BURROUGHS

SOLDIERS OF THE JUNGLE

NOW, WITH ONE SUPREME SURGE OF POWER, TARZAN COMPRESSED THE THROAT OF THE LIONESS. THE CHOKING BEAST FELL, CARRYING HER ANTAGONIST WITH HER

HER HEAD STRUCK THE GROUND SHARPLY, AND SHE LAY STILL, UNCONSCIOUS.

TARZAN RAN TO THE FIGHTING LETHOR AND BOHGDU. SHOUTING THREATS AND STERN COMMANDS HE PULLED THEM APART.

TO THE APE HE SAID: "LION IS MY FRIEND. YOU MY FRIEND. TARZAN'S ALLIES MUST FIGHT FOR TARZAN, NOT AGAINST EACH OTHER."

HE RETURNED TO THE LIONESS AND STROKED HER HEAD, BUT AS SHE REVIVED SHE ROSE WEAKLY TO RENEW THE ATTACK.

LETHOR CUFFED HER SMARTLY, THEN LICKED TARZAN'S FACE TO SHOW HE WAS THEIR FRIEND. THE LIONESS RELAXED.

MEANWHILE THE APES WERE OBSERVING THESE IMPRESSIVE EVENTS WITH ENCHANTED AWE.

"TARZAN IS MIGHTY," SAID ONE; "HE RULES FIERCE LIONS. HE SAVED OUR BALUS. HE IS OUR FRIEND."

HOGARTH-

"ME FIGHT FOR TARZAN," GROWLED A DOUGHTY APE WARRIOR. OTHERS GRUNTED APPROVAL, AND SOON HALF THE BULLS OF THE TRIBE VOLUNTEERED EACH BOASTING HIS PROWESS AS A FIGHTER.

TARZAN TURNED THEN TO MARCH AGAINST THE FOE, AND BEHIND HIM LUMBERED HIS STRANGE JUNGLE MILITIA.

NEXT WEEK: JUNGLE VENGEANCE

Tarzan

by Edgar Rice Burroughs

© 1937, Edgar Rice Burroughs, Inc. — Tm. Reg. U.S. Pat. Off.
Produced by Stephen Slesinger and Pfeuffer, Distributed by
UNITED FEATURE SYNDICATE, Inc.

JUNGLE VENGEANCE

WITH HIGH HOPES TARZAN LED HIS WARRIOR APES THROUGH THE FOREST TO ASSAIL THE FOE.

AND THAT NIGHT, WHILE THE ENEMY CAMP SLEPT, THE APE-MAN ASSIGNED THEM TO STATIONS IN THE TREES.

THEN A BIRD-LIKE CRY SHRILLED THROUGH THE JUNGLE. IT WAS TARZAN'S SIGNAL OF THE ZERO HOUR.

THE APES SWOOPED DOWN, AND SILENTLY THROTTLED THE SENTRIES. THEN THEY WERE FREE TO INVADE THE TENTS.

MANY A SOLDIER AWOKE TO FIND LEATHERY FINGERS AT HIS THROAT; AND MANY DIED WITHOUT A SOUND.

SOME, HOWEVER, WERE ABLE TO CRY OUT. THEIR BEWILDERED COMRADES SPRANG TO ARMS.

BUT AT THE FIRST ALARM, TARZAN VOICED THE APE-CRY OF WARNING, AND HIS RAIDERS FLED.

THEN FROM HIGH IN THE TREES THE JUNGLE LORD CALLED DOWN: "THE JUNGLE LAYS ITS VENGEFUL HAND UPON YOU!"

BELOW, EVEN THE BRAVEST TREMBLED AT THIS TERRIFYING THRUST OUT OF THE WILDERNESS

NEXT DAY, THE APES, BOASTING OF THEIR DEEDS, WERE EAGER TO REPEAT THEIR VICTORIOUS FORAY.

MEANWHILE, FLINT AND HIS STAFF PREPARED A PLAN OF DEFENSE AND DESTRUCTION AGAINST THE APE BATTALION.

AND WHEN TARZAN LED HIS HOST ONCE MORE TO THE FRAY, THEIR FOES WERE READY TO TRAP THEM!
NEXT WEEK: **HENCHMEN OF DEATH**

Tarzan
by EDGAR RICE BURROUGHS

HENCHMEN OF DEATH

CAMOUFLAGED RIFLEMEN AND MACHINE GUNNERS WERE *STATIONED* AT THE EDGE OF THE CAMP----- ---TO WATCH THE TREES AND POUR A DELUGE OF BULLETS INTO THE RANKS OF TARZAN'S JUNGLE RAIDERS.

TARZAN, KNOWING THE CAMP WOULD BE ALERT, LEFT HIS COMPANY OF APES AND SWUNG AHEAD TO RECONNOITRE.

AS HE NEARED HIS GOAL, HE GREW SUSPICIOUS OF THE UNNATURAL QUIET THAT HUNG OVER THE BIVOUAC.

TONIGHT NO SENTRIES PACED THEIR POSTS. SURELY THE CAMP WAS NOT UNGUARDED. SOMETHING WAS WRONG!

NOW TARZAN CAUGHT THE *SCENT* OF MANY MEN AT THE EDGE OF THE FOREST. SILENTLY HE EASED DOWNWARD.

THEN HE DISCOVERED THE TRAP—THE HIDDEN HENCHMEN OF DEATH. HE SLIPPED AWAY AND RETURNED TO THE APES.

THEY MUST AWAIT ANOTHER NIGHT, WHEN THE FOE WAS LESS WARY, HE EXPLAINED. THE APES GROWLED ANGRILY.

THEIR FIERCE BLOOD BOILED WITH BATTLE-LUST; NOR DID THEY UNDERSTAND THE POWER OF THE ENEMY'S WEAPONS.

INFLAMED BY LAST NIGHT'S VICTORY, THE STUBBORN APES CONSIDERED THEMSELVES INVINCIBLE WARRIORS.

"TARZAN IS AFRAID," ONE HOOTED; "WE GO ALONE." THEN ALL EXCEPT BOHGDU STORMED AWAY TO THE FRAY.

HOGARTH—

TARZAN FROWNED. HE WAS LOSING HIS ALLIES. THOSE WHO *SURVIVED* THE GUNS WOULD NEVER FOLLOW HIM AGAIN!

NEXT WEEK: **A DESPERATE CHANCE**

Tarzan

by Edgar Rice Burroughs

A DESPERATE CHANCE

WITH HEAVY HEART TARZAN WATCHED HIS BATTLE-CRAZED ALLIES SWING AWAY TO THEIR FOOLHARDY RAID.

THEY HAD IGNORED HIS WARNING, DISOBEYED HIS ORDERS, BUT HE COULD NOT STAND BY WHILE THEY SPED TO DISASTER.

HE MUST STOP THEM—OR TAKE COMMAND OF THE RIOTOUS BAND AND SAVE AS MANY AS HE COULD FROM SLAUGHTER.

WITH BOHGDU HE SPEEDILY OVERHAULED THE MAD APES, BUT NOTHING COULD SWAY THEM FROM THEIR RECKLESS PURPOSE.

"THEN I WILL LEAD YOU," THE APE MAN SAID; "THOUGH MANY OF US WILL DIE!"

AS THEY FOLLOWED HIM, TARZAN WRACKED HIS BRAIN FOR SOME STRATAGEM TO WARD OFF CERTAIN DEFEAT.

HE HIT UPON A SCHEME. HALTING NEAR THE ENEMY CAMP HE COMMANDED THE APES TO GATHER LONG, PLIANT LIANAS.

CARRYING THE VINES HE VENTURED CAUTIOUSLY INTO THE TREES IN THE CENTER OF THE ENEMY CAMP.

BELOW, THE SOLDIERS AWAITED ANY MOVEMENT IN THESE TREES WHICH MIGHT BETRAY THE EXPECTED RAIDERS.

THE APES GREW IMPATIENT, MYSTIFIED BY THE ACTIONS OF TARZAN, WHO---

---CALMLY PURSUED HIS STRANGE TASK OF TYING THE VINES TO BRANCHES OF THE TREES KNOWING THAT---

—IF HE MADE ONE MISSTEP, THE GUNS BELOW WOULD SPEAK WITH TONGUES OF DEATH!

HOGARTH—

NEXT WEEK: DARING ADVENTURE—

Tarzan

by Edgar Rice Burroughs

© 1937, Edgar Rice Burroughs, Inc.—Trade Mark U.S. Pat. Off.
Produced by Famous Books and Plays. Distributed by
UNITED FEATURE SYNDICATE, Inc.

DARING ADVENTURE

WHEN TARZAN HAD TIED THE VINES TO THE TREES, HE RETURNED CAUTIOUSLY TO THE PUZZLED APES.

TO ONE HE HANDED THE ENDS OF THE LIANAS, AND WITH THE OTHERS HE SLIPPED DOWN IN BACK OF THE CAMOUFLAGED SOLDIERS.

THEN, AS TARZAN HAD ORDERED, THE APE ABOVE TUGGED THE VINES, RUSTLING THE TREES IN THE CENTER OF THE CAMP.

THE EXCITED SOLDIERS OPENED FIRE, BELIEVING THE EXPECTED APE-RAID HAD BEGUN.

BUT WHILE THEY WERE THUS DISTRACTED, TARZAN AND HIS SAVAGE RAIDERS POUNCED UPON THEM FROM BEHIND.

AS THE JUNGLE LORD HAD INSTRUCTED, EACH APE ACCOUNTED FOR A MAN, THEN BEAT A HASTY RETREAT.

WHEN THE OTHER SOLDIERS RECOVERED FROM THEIR BEWILDERMENT, THE APES HAD VANISHED.

TARZAN'S TRIUMPH RENEWED THE LOYALTY OF THE APES, BUT HE KNEW THESE FORAYS WERE MERE PINPRICKS TO HIS POWERFUL FOES.

AS HE CONSIDERED HOW HE MIGHT WIN NEW ALLIES FOR AN OVERWHELMING MASS ATTACK, A STARTLING THOUGHT CAME TO HIM.

TO THE SOUTH LAY LION COUNTRY. IF HE COULD MASTER THOSE WILD BEASTS AND MOLD THEM INTO A FIGHTING FORCE—! FROM THE FOREST HE CALLED LETHOR AND HIS MATE TO ACCOMPANY HIM. THEN HE HEADED SOUTHWARD.

HOGARTH-

MIGHTY WAS TARZAN, LORD OF THE JUNGLE, BUT WAS THIS NEW TASK MIGHTIER THAN HE?
NEXT WEEK: *THE LION TRAP*

24   Tarzan in the City of Gold

Tarzan
by EDGAR RICE BURROUGHS

THE LION TRAP

ON A PARCHED PLAIN HE ENCOUNTERED HERDS OF ANTELOPES, MIGRATING TO FRESH GRAZING GROUND.

TARZAN TREKKED SOUTHWARD, TO ATTEMPT THE AMAZING FEAT OF MASTERING AND TRAINING A PACK OF WILD LIONS FOR HIS JUNGLE ARMY. HE TRAVELED SWIFTLY, LEAVING LETHOR AND LOYYA, HIS LION FRIENDS, TO TRAIL HIM LIKE FAITHFUL DOGS.

AND SOON THE SHIFTING BREEZE BROUGHT HIM THE SCENT OF MANY LIONS, FOLLOWING THE WALKING FOOD SUPPLY.

SUDDENLY, FROM BEHIND A HILLOCK, SIX OF THE CARNIVORES ROSE UP, SNARLING ANGRILY AT THE INTRUDER.

TARZAN SPOKE TO THEM SOFTLY, BUT ON THEY CAME. HE GROWLED THREATENINGLY, STILL ON THEY CAME.

AT LAST HE WAS FORCED TO FLEE TO REFUGE IN A TREE, FOR HE COULD NOT FIGHT THEM ALL.

HOURS LATER, LETHOR AND LOYYA APPEARED. THEY SAW HIS PLIGHT, AND CHARGED HIS JAILORS.

TARZAN ORDERED THEM BACK, BUT THEY DID NOT HEAR: THEY WERE LIKE EXCITED DOGS RACING TO AID THEIR MASTER.

SAVAGELY THE OTHER LIONS MET THE UNNATURAL ATTACK.

SEEING THAT HIS ALLIES WOULD BE DESTROYED, TARZAN DROPPED DOWN TO AID THEM.

HOGARTH—

AND IMMEDIATELY FOUR OF THE HOSTILE BEASTS DARTED TOWARD HIM!

NEXT WEEK: FRIENDS--OR FOES?

Tarzan
by Edgar Rice Burroughs

Copr. 1937, Edgar Rice Burroughs, Inc.—Reg. U.S. Pat.
Off. Produced by Famous Books and Plays. Distributed by
UNITED FEATURE SYNDICATE, Inc.

FRIENDS--OR FOES?

WHEN THE LIONS CHARGED, TARZAN FLED. HE COULD NOT HOPE TO CONQUER ALL FOUR.

BUT HE WANTED TO DRAW THEM OFF WHILE HIS FAITHFUL LETHOR AND LOYYA FOUGHT TWO OF THEIR FELLOWS.

ACROSS THE PLAIN DASHED TARZAN, WITH THE BEASTS IN FURIOUS PURSUIT.

AS HE SURMOUNTED A HILLOCK, THE SIGHT OF AN ANTELOPE HERD INSPIRED A STARTLING PLAN.

HE OVERHAULED ONE OF THE ANIMALS, KILLED IT, AND FLUNG THE CARCASS IN THE PATH OF THE RACING LIONS.

THE PURSUERS HALTED, FOR THEY COULD NOT RESIST THIS TASTY FEAST WHICH CAME TO THEM SO EASILY.

TARZAN MIGHT HAVE ESCAPED; INSTEAD HE MADE ANOTHER KILL AND TOSSED IT TO THE LIONS.

SLOWLY HE APPROACHED THEM, AND THEY MADE NO MOVE AGAINST THE STRANGE MAN-THING WHO HAD SUPPLIED THEIR FEAST.

THE BEASTS GORGED AND BECAME LAZY AND SLEEPY. TARZAN SPOKE GENTLY. HE WAS RESOLVED TO ENLIST THEM IN HIS JUNGLE ARMY.

TARZAN WALKED FEARLESSLY AMONG THEM, LETTING THEM SNIFF HIM, AND SHOWING HE MEANT NO HARM. BUT NOW---

THE VICTORIOUS LETHOR AND LOYYA RACED OVER THE HILL. THE WILD LIONS BRISTLED AND ROARED.

HOGARTH—

THEIR EXCITEMENT, TARZAN KNEW, MIGHT BREAK THE SPELL AND UNLEASH THEIR UNREASONING SAVAGERY AGAINST HIM.

NEXT WEEK: *KING OF THE LIONS*

Tarzan
by Edgar Rice Burroughs

KING OF THE LIONS

AS LETHOR AND LOYYA RACED TOWARD THE WILD LIONS, TARZAN SHOUTED "HALT!" AND THEY OBEYED.

THE JUNGLE LORD WISHED TO MAKE PEACE AMONG THEM, SO THAT ALL MIGHT BE HIS FRIENDS AND SERVE HIS PURPOSE.

HE HASTENED TO LETHOR AND LOYYA. THEY WELCOMED HIM WITH SOFT PURRS, AND FOLLOWED HIM BACK.

THE WILD LIONS GROWLED AND IN TARZAN'S THROAT RUMBLED AN ANSWERING GROWL, FIERCE AND POSITIVE

THE BEWILDERED BRUTES SUBSIDED, FOR THEY FELT THE POWER AND KINGSHIP OF THIS CREATURE WHO WAS BOTH MAN AND BEAST.

NOW, WITH A MIXTURE OF FIRMNESS AND KINDNESS, TARZAN SOUGHT TO BEND THEM TO HIS WILL.

AND SLOWLY FROM THE WILDERNESS, HE DREW MORE RECRUITS, AND TRAINED THEM TO HIS COMMAND.

HE HUNTED WITH THEM, AND PROVED HIMSELF THE MIGHTIEST HUNTER OF THEM ALL. HE BECAME KING OF THE KINGS OF BEASTS.

AFTER SEVERAL WEEKS, TARZAN WAS CAPTAIN OF A LARGE COMPANY OF SOLDIER-LIONS.

THEN HE STARTED NORTH, TO HURL THIS SAVAGE JUNGLE ARMY AGAINST HIS HUMAN FOES. BUT AS THEY WERE PASSING THROUGH A VALLEY, A WILD TRUMPETING CAME TO TARZAN'S EARS, AND PRESENTLY----

----A HERD OF ELEPHANTS THUNDERED TOWARD THEM IN MAD STAMPEDE! NEXT WEEK: CHALLENGE!

HOGARTH—

Tarzan

by Edgar Rice Burroughs

CHALLENGE

IN FURIOUS STAMPEDE, THE ELEPHANTS SWEPT DOWN THE NARROW VALLEY.

TARZAN TRIED HASTILY TO DIVERT HIS ARMY OF LIONS FROM THE PATH OF THE RAMPAGE. BUT THE LIONS, FIGHTERS BY INSTINCT, ROARED ACCEPTANCE OF WHAT THEY BELIEVED WAS A CHALLENGE.

THE ELEPHANTS HAD NO WISH TO FIGHT, BUT THEY WOULD CRUSH ANY OBSTACLE THAT BLOCKED THEM.

THE LIONS DARTED FORWARD. MOST OF THEM TARZAN STOPPED, BUT A FEW PLUNGED ON, AND--

---HURLED THEMSELVES RECKLESSLY ON THE VANGUARD OF THE LUMBERING HERD.

BUT THEY WERE TRAMPLED AND GORED, AND DASHED ASIDE BY THE IMPACT OF POWERFUL TUSKS. NOW THE OTHER LIONS, MADDENED BY SIGHT OF THE CONFLICT, RACED FORWARD.

TARZAN WAS DISMAYED, FOR HE WAS LOATH TO LOSE HIS ARMY OF SOLDIER LIONS.

HE RESOLVED UPON A DESPERATE PLAN. LEAPING TREEWARD, HE SPED TOWARD THE HERD OF MAMMOTHS.

HE REACHED THEM WELL AHEAD OF THE SECOND WAVE OF LIONS-----

HOGARTH--

--AND DROPPED DOWN ON THE BACK OF THE LEADER!

NEXT WEEK:
A FRIEND IN NEED

Tarzan

by EDGAR RICE BURROUGHS

A FRIEND IN NEED

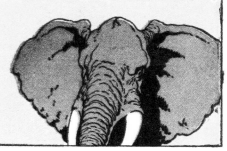

AS TARZAN ALIGHTED ON HIS BACK, THE LEADER OF THE STAMPEDING ELEPHANTS BELLOWED AND SWUNG HIS TRUNK.

THEN THE APE-MAN OBSERVED A GREAT SCAR ON THE BEAST'S HEAD. THIS WAS TANTOR, FRIEND OF HIS YOUTH!

EVENTS HAD BEEN FLASHING TOO RAPIDLY FOR HIM TO IDENTIFY THE ELEPHANT BEFORE. NOW HE SHOUTED HAPPILY: "TANTOR!"

THE BIG BEAST TRUMPETED JOYOUSLY AT THE SOUND OF THAT FAMILIAR VOICE, FOR OF ALL CREATURES HE LOVED TARZAN BEST.

NOW TANTOR'S FEARS WERE LULLED. HE HALTED AT TARZAN'S COMMAND, AND HIS FOLLOWERS HALTED, TOO.

BUT THE LIONS PRESSED ON IN THEIR FRENZIED CHARGE.

TARZAN LEAPED DOWN AND TOOK A FIRM STANCE IN FRONT OF THEM, BUT ON THEY CAME!

THE LEADER, HAVING NO WISH TO HARM THE MAN-THING WHO WAS HIS FRIEND, TRIED TO LEAP OVER HIM.

BUT TARZAN CAUGHT THE BEAST IN MIDAIR, AND FLUNG HIM INTO THE DASHING PACK.

THE SHOCK BROUGHT THEM TO THEIR SENSES, AND THEY STOPPED AT THEIR MASTER'S SHOUTED COMMAND.

THEN TARZAN REMOUNTED TANTOR, WHEELED HIM ABOUT, AND HEADED NORTH AGAIN. NOW HE WAS READY TO PIT----

--THE MIGHTIEST AND FIERCEST FORCES OF THE JUNGLE AGAINST HIS "CIVILIZED" FOES!
NEXT WEEK: **TARZAN'S LAST STAND**

Tarzan

by Edgar Rice Burroughs

TARZAN'S LAST STAND

PACED BY THE ELEPHANTS' MEASURED TREAD, TARZAN'S JUNGLE ARMY MOVED ON TO BATTLE.

A FEW DAYS LATER, HE EFFECTED A JUNCTION WITH HIS COMPANY OF FIGHTING APES.

MEANWHILE, THE BIG RAINS HAD BOGGED FLINT'S MECHANIZED BATTALIONS IN A SEA OF MUD.

BUT AT LAST THE DOWNPOURS CEASED, THE SUN SHONE HOT, THE EARTH DRIED, AND THE ARMY PUSHED ON AGAIN.

TARZAN, SCOUTING AHEAD, SAW HIS FOES MOVING TOWARD THE PASS WHICH WAS THE GATEWAY TO THE GOLDEN CITY.

THAT NIGHT FLINT CAMPED ON THE PLAIN, IN A POSITION THAT WAS TOO OPEN FOR A SURPRISE ATTACK.

SO THE APE-MAN SKIRTED WIDE AND LED HIS WARRIOR BEASTS INTO THE PASS.

THERE HE DISTRIBUTED THEM AT STRATEGIC POINTS, BEHIND BOULDERS AND CLUMPS OF SCRAWNY BUSHES.

THEN WITH THE ELEPHANTS HE BLOCKED THE PASS, AND WAITED---- READY FOR A LAST, DESPERATE STAND.

NEAR NOON, THE VAN-GUARD OF THE TANKS RUMBLED OMINOUSLY AROUND THE CURVE.

"CHARGE!" TARZAN SHOUTED; AND THE GIANTS OF THE JUNGLE DASHED FORWARD....TO ENGAGE THOSE MAN-MADE MONSTERS WITH HIDES OF STEEL!

NEXT WEEK: *THE WAR OF THE WORLDS*

Tarzan

by EDGAR RICE BURROUGHS

THE WAR OF TWO WORLDS

TARZAN HAD NO NEED TO URGE THE ELEPHANTS TO BATTLE THEY WERE INFURIATED BY THE CHALLENGING IRON MONSTERS

SO THE JUNGLE LORD LEAPED DOWN AND COMMANDED THE EXCITED LIONS TO CHARGE.

ALREADY THE FIGHTING APES WERE POUNCING FURIOUSLY UPON THE CONVOY OF TRUCKS

WHILE THE TERROR-STRICKEN TANKMEN FUMBLED TREMBLINGLY AT THE MACHINE-GUNS---

-THE WAVE OF JUNGLE GIANTS STRUCK THE ARMORED MACHINES AND TOPPLED THEM INTO THE CANYON

THEN IN A FRENZY OF DESTRUCTION THEY SMASHED INTO THE TRUCKS

THE FEW BULLETS THEY RECEIVED IN THEIR TOUGH HIDES MERELY INFLAMED THEIR FURY

AND IN THE REAR, THE LIONS WERE TAKING A TERRIBLE TOLL THE SOLDIERS WERE SO COMPRESSED IN PANICKY CONFUSION THAT THEIR WEAPONS WERE ALMOST USELESS.

TARZAN WAS IN THE MIDST OF THE BATTLE FOR HE, NO LESS THAN THE LIONS, WAS A FIGHTING JUNGLE BEAST.

BUT NOW AN ARTILLERY CAPTAIN MANAGED TO RALLY A CREW AND UNLIMBER A GUN.

IF HE COULD BLAST THE WAVE OF ELEPHANTS, HE STILL MIGHT TURN THE TIDE OF BATTLE!

NEXT WEEK: *STAMPEDE*

Tarzan
by EDGAR RICE BURROUGHS

Copt 1937 Edgar Rice Burroughs, Inc.—The Reg. U.S. Pat.
Off. Produced by Famous Books and Plays. Distributing by
UNITED FEATURE SYNDICATE, Inc.

STAMPEDE

IN DISMAY TARZAN SAW THE FIELD GUN PREPARED TO BLAST HIS ELEPHANT WARRIORS INTO OBLIVION.

WITH A SHOUT HE SUMMONED SEVERAL OF HIS APES, AND TOGETHER-----

------THEY POUNCED FIERCELY UPON THE GUNNERS, JUST AS THEY WERE READY TO FIRE.

AND THE ELEPHANTS SWEPT SAFELY PAST, TO CONTINUE THEIR MISSION OF MAD DESTRUCTION.

NOW TARZAN'S BAND OF TAANORIANS, WHO HAD LONG AWAITED HIS RETURN, HEARD THE DIN OF BATTLE FROM AFAR.

THEY HURRIED TOWARD THE FRAY, AND TARZAN FLUNG THEM INTO THE RAGING CONFLICT.

RAPIDLY THE MEN AND MACHINES OF CIVILIZATION GAVE WAY BEFORE THE MIGHTY ONSLAUGHT OF JUNGLE FORCES,

...AND VICTORY SETTLED ON TARZAN'S BANNER!

IN HIS ARMORED CAR, RUFUS FLINT, THE CRUEL LEADER OF THE INVADERS, COMMANDED HIS DRIVER TO TURN AND FLEE.

BUT NOW TARZAN DIRECTED HIS ELEPHANTS AGAINST THE CAR. THEY STRUCK IT WITH TERRIFIC FORCE.

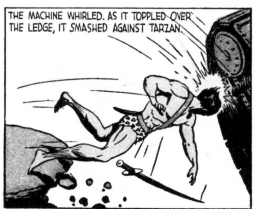

THE MACHINE WHIRLED. AS IT TOPPLED OVER THE LEDGE, IT SMASHED AGAINST TARZAN.

UNCONSCIOUS, THE APE-MAN HURTLED INTO THE DEEP CANYON, AND THE GROUND RUSHED UP TO CLAIM HIM!

NEXT WEEK: CABIN IN THE WILDERNESS

HOGARTH.—

Tarzan

by EDGAR RICE BURROUGHS

CABIN IN THE WILDERNESS

TWISTING AND TURNING, THE UNCONSCIOUS TARZAN PLUNGED INTO THE STREAM BELOW.

THE TAANORIANS WERE CERTAIN HE WAS DEAD. AND NOW THAT THEIR FOES WERE DESTROYED, THEY HASTENED HOMEWARD.

IN THE GOLDEN CITY, THE JOY OF VICTORY WAS MINGLED WITH GRIEF FOR HIM WHO HAD GIVEN HIS LIFE FOR THEIR FREEDOM.

QUEEN NAKONIA WEPT UNASHAMED; THEN BRAVELY TOOK UP THE TASK OF RESTORING HER HARASSED LAND.

BUT TARZAN WAS NOT DEAD. SWIFT WATERS WHIRLED HIM ONTO A MASS OF DEBRIS AND BORE HIM DOWNSTREAM.

WHEN HE REGAINED HIS SENSES HE WAS FAR AWAY. HE STARTED BACK TO THE BATTLEFIELD. BUT WHY RETURN?

THE INVADERS WERE ERASED; HIS MISSION HAD BEEN FULFILLED; JUSTICE WAS DONE. AND HE PICTURED......

----HIS STRANGE ARMY OF BEASTS DISSOLVING INTO THE VAST WILDERNESS WHENCE THEY CAME.

SO TARZAN JOURNEYED SOUTHWARD, BY DEVIOUS TRAILS AS FANCY PROMPTED. ONE DAY HE CAME UPON A WEATHER-BEATEN CABIN ON A WILD SEACOAST.

HE STOPPED SHORT, ENTRANCED; A THOUSAND MEMORIES THRONGED HIS MIND. THIS WAS THE CABIN OF HIS BIRTH. HERE HIS MAROONED PARENTS, LORD AND LADY GREYSTOKE HAD PERISHED.

HERE, AS AN INFANT, HE HAD BEEN ADOPTED BY KALA, THE SHE-APE.

SUDDENLY TARZAN'S REVERIE WAS INTERRUPTED BY A HOSTILE VOICE, A HARSH INHUMAN VOICE-- CALLING HIS NAME.

NEXT WEEK: TARZAN'S HOME-COMING

HOGARTH—

Tarzan

by EDGAR RICE BURROUGHS

344 - 10-10

TARZAN'S HOMECOMING

WHEN HE HEARD A GUTTURAL VOICE CALLING HIS NAME, TARZAN TURNED AND SAW A GREAT APE HIGH IN THE TREES.

"CHAKTO!" HE CRIED HAPPILY, FOR THIS WAS AN APE OF THE TRIBE THAT HAD REARED HIM FROM INFANCY.

BUT CHAKTO SNARLED. "WHEN TARZAN OUR KING, WE SAFE. THEN TARZAN GO AWAY; BEASTS AND BLACK MAN KILL US. TARZAN DOES NOT HELP US!"

"TARZAN WILL KILL ENEMIES OF OUR TRIBE," THE APE-MAN GROWLED. CHAKTO GRUNTED AND GUIDED HIM TOWARD HIS FELLOWS.

FOR TARZAN THE JOURNEY TURNED BACK THE PAGES OF TIME AND HE LIVED AGAIN THE MATCHLESS SAGA OF HIS YOUTH.

IN THOSE TREES YONDER, HE HAD LEARNED TO SWING AND FLY FROM BOUGH TO BOUGH LIKE THE GREAT APES THEMSELVES.

OVER THERE, AS A BOY, HE WAS GRAVELY WOUNDED IN VICTORIOUS BATTLE WITH BOLGANI, THE GIANT GORILLA.

HERE, AS A YOUTH, HE WON THE KINGSHIP OF THE APE-TRIBE BY KILLING KERCHAK, THE CHALLENGING MONARCH.

IN THIS FOREST HE BLENDED HIS HUMAN AND ANIMAL TRAITS-TO BECOME SUPER-BEAST AND SUPER-MAN, THE MIGHTY LORD OF THE JUNGLE.

TARZAN WAS HOME; AND HE GREETED HIS FOSTER PEOPLE HAPPILY; BUT THEY ANSWERED WITH SULLEN, HOSTILE GRUNTS.

THEN ONE STEPPED FORWARD. HE WAS TALUG, A FRIEND OF TARZAN'S BOYHOOD; BUT HE WAS NO FRIEND NOW.

HOGARTH—

"TALUG IS KING," HE GROWLED JEALOUSLY; "IF TARZAN COMES TO BE KING AGAIN, TARZAN MUST FIGHT TALUG. TALUG KILL!"
NEXT WEEK: TARZAN'S EXILE

Tarzan
by EDGAR RICE BURROUGHS

TARZAN'S EXILE

AS TAUG BARKED HIS CHALLENGE TO TARZAN, A SHRIEK OF TERROR BURST FROM THE EDGE OF THE CLEARING. THE APE-MAN TURNED---

--TO SEE A GREAT LION LEAP FROM THE THICKET, STRIKE DOWN A HALF-GROWN APE, AND FLEE WITH HIS LIFELESS PREY.

"WE KILL THE LION," TARZAN SHOUTED. TAUG GRUNTED. "WHY RISK OUR LIVES? MIKKA ALREADY DEAD."

BUT THE APE-MAN'S HUMAN FORESIGHT TOLD HIM THAT IF THE LION SUCCEEDED NOW, HE WOULD REPEAT HIS RAID.

SO TARZAN GAVE CHASE; AND LAUNCHED HIMSELF AT THE LION'S BACK-A HAZARDOUS TECHNIQUE HE HAD PERFECTED IN HIS BOYHOOD.

THE LION REARED AND SHOOK, BUT TARZAN'S KNIFE STRUCK AGAIN AND AGAIN, UNTIL THE TAWNY BEAST FELL DEAD.

THEN THE JUNGLE LORD PLACED A FOOT UPON THE CARCASS, AND FROM HIS THROAT ISSUED THE AWFUL APE-CRY OF VICTORY.

THEN CAME THE APES, SOME GRUNTING APPROVAL; BUT TAUG PUFFED WITH JEALOUS ANGER. "TARZAN GO, OR TAUG KILL!"

"TARZAN DOES NOT FIGHT HIS OWN PEOPLE," THE APE-MAN ANSWERED. THEN HE TURNED AND STALKED AWAY.

A STRANGE SADNESS FILLED HIM, FOR NOW HE WAS EXILED BY THE COMPANIONS OF HIS YOUTH, HIS COUSINS OF THE JUNGLE.

SUDDENLY, THE FOREST RESOUNDED WITH THE GUTTURAL SHRIEKS OF APES AND THE EXCITED CRIES OF SAVAGE MEN

NEXT WEEK: SAVAGE RAIDERS -

HOGARTH-

THE APES WERE IN TROUBLE! AND THOUGH THEY HAD SPURNED HIM, TARZAN RACED TO AID THEM, AT THE PERIL OF HIS LIFE!

Tarzan
by EDGAR RICE BURROUGHS

SAVAGE RAIDERS

WILD CRIES INFORMED TARZAN THAT THE BLACKS WERE PURSUING THEIR FAVORITE SPORT OF HUNTING DOWN THE APES.

BUT HE CAME TOO LATE. THE BLACKS HAD VANISHED, LEAVING HAVOC AMONG THE "HAIRY MEN OF THE FOREST."

"THE GOMANGANI TOOK TAUG PRISONER," A BIG BULL SHOUTED; "NOW TARZAN IS OUR KING AGAIN!"

THE APE MAN SHOOK HIS HEAD. "I SHALL BRING TAUG BACK." THEN HE DARTED AWAY THROUGH THE TREES.

SOON HE OVERHAULED THE RAIDERS, AND SURVEYED THEM WITH SCORN AND HATRED, FOR THESE WERE MEN OF MBONGA'S TRIBE. ONE OF THESE VICIOUS CANNIBALS HAD LONG AGO SLAIN KALA, HIS APE FOSTER MOTHER. SINCE THEN HE HAD BEEN THEIR UNRELENTING FOE.

POOR TAUG WAS SHRIEKING AND BEATING AGAINST THE BARS OF THE CAGE, WHILE THE BLACK MEN HOWLED WITH GLEE.

TO THE KRAAL THEY BORE HIM AND THE VILLAGERS TORTURED THE HELPLESS BEAST AND GOADED HIM TO MADNESS.

DUSK FELL, AND THE CAGE WAS PLACED BENEATH TWO TREES, WHILE THE SAVAGES QUAFFED NATIVE BEER.

SOON THEY BEGAN THEIR FRENZIED DANCE OF VICTORY, RE-ENACTING THEIR BATTLE WITH THE APES.

THEN THE ROPES WERE MADE READY TO DRAG THE ILL-FATED TAUG TO SLAUGHTER.

HOGARTH—

TARZAN HAD TO ACT NOW OR NEVER. HE HAD TO PIT HIS LONE HAND AGAINST THE SAVAGE HORDE!
NEXT WEEK: *THE DEVIL-GOD*

Tarzan
by Edgar Rice Burroughs

THE DEVIL-GOD

TARZAN KNEW IT WOULD BE FATAL TO TRY TO SAVE TAUG FROM THE SAVAGES BY FORCE.

BUT PRESENTLY, ON THE ROOF OF A HUT, HE SPIED THE SKIN OF AN APE, A TROPHY OF SOME FORMER RAID.

TARZAN DROPPED DOWN, CREPT WARILY THROUGH THE SHADOWS, AND ENVELOPED HIMSELF IN THE SHAGGY PELT.

THEN HE LEAPED FORWARD. THE BLACKS WERE ASTOUNDED. HAD SOME DEMON HELPED THE GREAT APE TO FLEE HIS CAGE?

QUICKLY, HOWEVER, THEY RECOVERED FROM THEIR SHOCK. "KILL!" THE CHIEFTAIN SHOUTED.

THEN THE APE-MAN SHED THE SKIN. "BEWARE!" HE THUNDERED. "THE MIGHTY TARZAN HAS RETURNED." THE SAVAGES SHRANK BACK.

THEY HAD REASON TO FEAR TARZAN, BECAUSE IN FORMER YEARS HE HAD PLAGUED AND MYSTIFIED THEM BY FEATS OF POWER AND CUNNING.

"THE DEVIL-GOD!" THEY SHRIEKED; "HE CHANGES FROM APE TO MAN." AND WHILE CONFUSION GRIPPED THEM—

—TARZAN DASHED AWAY TO RELEASE TAUG; "FOLLOW ME" HE COMMANDED, AND RACED TOWARD THE PALISADE.

BUT TAUG'S SMALL BRAIN HAD ROOM FOR ONLY ONE IDEA— TO SHED THE BLOOD OF THOSE WHO HAD TORTURED HIM.

WHEN TARZAN SAW THE FRENZIED APE CHARGE THE SAVAGES, HE TURNED TO FOLLOW.

HOGARTH—

TARZAN COULD NEVER DESERT A COMRADE THOUGH DEATH ITSELF BE THE PRICE OF HIS LOYALTY.

NEXT WEEK: TARZAN THE BEAST

Tarzan and the Boers, Part I   37

Tarzan

by EDGAR RICE BURROUGHS

Copr. 1951, Edgar Rice Burroughs, Inc.—Tm. Reg. U. S. Pat.
Off. Produced by Famous Books and Plays. Distributed by
UNITED FEATURE SYNDICATE, Inc.

TARZAN THE BEAST

TARZAN THRILLED TO THE DESPERATE BATTLE AS HE FOUGHT BESIDE HIS HAIRY COMPANION.

DEFEAT, HOWEVER, WAS CERTAIN, SO HE CALLED TO TAUG TO FLEE; BUT THE BLOOD-MAD APE WAS DEAF TO PERSUASION.

THEN TARZAN'S JUNGLE LORE CAME TO HIS AID. HE KNEW THE APES' INSTINCT FOR IMITATION.

SO HE SEIZED ONE OF HIS ADVERSARIES AND LEAPED TREEWARD. TAUG COPIED HIS ACTIONS.

THEN THEY DASHED AWAY THROUGH THE TREES EACH BEARING A CAPTIVE TO THE APE-TRIBE.

TARZAN WAS GREETED WITH HOARSE ACCLAIM, BUT HE, IN TURN, VOICED PRAISE FOR TAUG AS A MIGHTY FIGHTER.

NOW THE EXCITED APES CLAMORED FOR A DUM-DUM, THAT GHASTLY RITE WHICH WAS A PRELUDE TO SLAUGHTERING CAPTIVES.

PRESENTLY THE BOOM OF THE EARTHDRUM RESOUNDED THROUGH THE JUNGLE, WEIRD AND TERRIBLE.

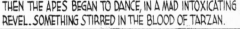

THEN THE APES BEGAN TO DANCE, IN A MAD INTOXICATING REVEL..SOMETHING STIRRED IN THE BLOOD OF TARZAN.

OFTEN AS A BOY, WHEN HE LIVED THE LIFE OF THE APES, HE HAD SHARED IN THESE CARNIVALS OF DEATH.

AND NOW THESE MAGIC DRUMBEATS CARRIED HIM BACK THROUGH THE YEARS. HE WAS A BEAST AGAIN! HOGARTH—

AND SO, WITH A BLOOD-CURDLING CRY, TARZAN JOINED THE WILD LEAPING HORDE-AS SAVAGE AS ANY APE!
NEXT WEEK: A MYSTERIOUS MESSENGER

349-11-14

Tarzan

by EDGAR RICE BURROUGHS

Copr. 1937. Edgar Rice Burroughs, Inc.—Tm. Reg. U.S. Pat.
Off. produced by Famous Books and Plays. Distributed by
UNITED FEATURE SYNDICATE, Inc.

A MYSTERIOUS MESSENGER

SHOUTING MADLY, TARZAN DANCED THE DEATH DANCE OF THE DUM-DUM AS SAVAGELY AS HIS FELLOW BEASTS!

SOON TWO OF THE SHAGGY APES TOOK UP CLUBS AND LUMBERED TOWARD THE DOOMED CAPTIVES.

SUDDENLY TARZAN SHOOK OFF THE HYPNOTIC SPELL; AND NOW THIS HIDEOUS REVEL FILLED HIM WITH DISMAY.

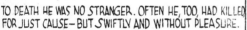

TO DEATH HE WAS NO STRANGER. OFTEN HE, TOO, HAD KILLED FOR JUST CAUSE—BUT SWIFTLY AND WITHOUT PLEASURE.

THOUGH HE HAD BEEN REARED BY THE APES, HE WAS A MAN OF NOBLE HERITAGE; HE COULD NOT SHARE IN THIS BRUTAL ORGY. BUT HE WAS TOO WISE TO ATTEMPT TO IMPOSE HIS OWN CODE UPON THE BRUTE INSTINCTS OF THE APES.

SO HE SLIPPED AWAY UNNOTICED INTO THE JUNGLE, UNOBSERVED BY THE BLOOD-MAD APES.

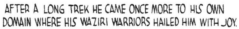

AFTER A LONG TREK HE CAME ONCE MORE TO HIS OWN DOMAIN WHERE HIS WAZIRI WARRIORS HAILED HIM WITH JOY.

BUT FOR TARZAN THERE WAS NO REST. ONE DAY A STRANGE MESSENGER CAME FROM ISHTAK, A CHIEF OF THE FAR SOUTH.

"EVIL WHITE MEN COME TO KILL US AND STEAL OUR LAND," HE SAID; "AND WE ASK THE AID OF MIGHTY TARZAN."

THE APE-MAN ANSWERED QUIETLY: "WHERE TARZAN IS NEEDED, TARZAN GOES." AND HE FOLLOWED THE COURIER SOUTHWARD——

HOGARTH—

——TOWARD THE AFRICAN VELDT. BUT HE MIGHT HAVE PAUSED HAD HE SEEN THE SLY SMILE OF TRIUMPH ON THE MESSENGER'S EVIL FACE
NEXT WEEK: SINISTER ALLIES

350-11-21

Tarzan
by Edgar Rice Burroughs

SINISTER ALLIES

FEARLESSLY TARZAN FOLLOWED THE EVIL-LOOKING MESSENGER, FOR THOSE PEOPLE HE HAD PROMISED TO FIGHT.

HE INQUIRED ABOUT THE WHITE MARAUDERS WHO THREATENED THE TRIBE, BUT THE COURIER ANSWERED VAGUELY.

AT LAST HE CAME TO THE LAND OF CHIEF ISHTAK, WHO RECEIVED HIM WITH A DISPLAY OF FRIENDSHIP WHICH WAS ONLY A MASK.

TARZAN PERCEIVED THAT THE CHIEF WAS A TYRANT OF KEEN MIND, STRONG WILL--AND SLY CUNNING.

HE DISLIKED ISHTAK, BUT HE WOULD NOT ALLOW HIS PREJUDICE TO SWERVE HIM FROM HIS PROMISED ALLIANCE. "TOMORROW," THE CHIEFTAIN GRINNED; "THE MIGHTY TARZAN WILL LEAD US AGAINST THE EVIL INVADERS."

AND WHILE ISHTAK MADE READY FOR THE BATTLE, THE APE-MAN INSPECTED THE VILLAGE OF THIS UNFAMILIAR PEOPLE.

HE FOUND AMONG THEM MUCH GOLD, AND MANY MODERN HAND-AXES WHICH SHOWED THAT THEY TRADED WITH THE WHITES.

AND WHEN HE WENT AMONG THE WARRIORS HE SENSED A SUBTLE UNDERCURRENT OF MYSTERY THAT HE COULD NOT FATHOM.

NEXT DAY, AS THE WAR PARTY MARCHED TOWARD THE PLAIN, ISHTAK WHISPERED TO HIS AIDE: "WITH TARZAN AS OUR LEADER WE SHALL KILL ALL THE WHITES."

HOGARTH-

"AYE," NODDED THE WARRIOR --"AND DEAD MEN CANNOT SPEAK; TARZAN WILL NEVER KNOW THE TRUTH!" NEXT WEEK: TREACHERY

Tarzan

by EDGAR RICE BURROUGHS

Page 1935 Edgar Rice Burroughs, Inc.—Tm. Reg. U.S. Pat.
Off. Distributed by Feature Books and Print Syndicate by
UNITED FEATURE SYNDICATE, Inc.

TREACHERY

----A LONG WAGON TRAIN CRAWLING LIKE A COLOSSAL SERPENT THROUGH THE ROLLING VELDT.

NEXT DAY, TARZAN AND THE WARRIORS CAME DOWN FROM THE FORESTED MOUNTAINS AND SAW IN THE DISTANCE------

"THEY," SNARLED ISHTAK, "ARE THE INVADERS WHO COME TO STEAL OUR LANDS. THEY MUST DIE!"

TIRELESSLY THE TREKKERS MOVED ON, STAUNCH AND STALWART, FOR THEY WERE CAST IN THE HEROIC MOLD OF PIONEERS.

LONG YEARS AGO THEIR BOER FOREFATHERS HAD CARVED A PASTORAL EMPIRE FROM THE WILDERNESS, AND NOW THESE SIMPLE, STURDY FOLK WERE PUSHING ON AGAIN TO ESCAPE THE NORTHWARD MARCH OF A STIFLING CIVILIZATION.

IN THE VANGUARD RODE JAN VAN BOEREN, STOUT PATRIARCH AND LEADER OF THE VENTURESOME BAND.

OLD JAN SMILED. "NOW WE HAVE COME TO OUR NEW COUNTRY. IT IS A FAIR LAND, AND WE SHALL BE HAPPY HERE."

BUT AT THAT MOMENT ISHTAK WAS PLANNING THEIR DOOM. "TONIGHT WE SHALL FALL UPON THEM---WITHOUT MERCY!"

"NO!" THE APE-MAN FROWNED. "TARZAN KILLS ONLY WHEN OTHER MEANS FAIL. I SHALL WARN THEM TO GO BACK."

ISHTAK TRIED TO DISSUADE HIM, BUT TARZAN SET OUT TOWARD THE TRAVELLERS. ISHTAK WHISPERED TO HIS AIDES:

"IF HE SPEAKS WITH THE WHITES, HE WILL DISCOVER OUR PLOT. TARZAN MUST NOT REACH THEM ALIVE."

NEXT WEEK: *BETWEEN TWO FIRES*

Tarzan

by EDGAR RICE BURROUGHS

BETWEEN TWO FIRES

AS TARZAN DEPARTED, ISHTAK COMMANDED; "ARCHERS! KILL HIM!" THEN BOW STRINGS SNAPPED. ARROWS WHIRRED.

THE APE-MAN WAS SHOCKED TO FIND HIMSELF THE TARGET OF THOSE WHO POSED AS HIS FRIENDS.

BUT HIS SURPRISE DID NOT CHECK HIS AGILITY. DARTING AND DODGING, HE SPED QUICKLY OUT OF RANGE.

ACROSS THE PLAIN HE FLED, LIKE A NIMBLE ANTELOPE, TOWARD THE WAGON TRAIN. DESPITE ISHTAK'S PUZZLING TREACHERY, HE WAS RESOLVED TO PREVENT THE THEFT OF THE BLACK CHIEF'S LANDS, IF THEFT IT TRULY WAS.

WHEN JAN VAN BOEREN SAW HIM, HE FINGERED HIS MUSKET. ON THE WILD FRONTIER IT WAS WELL TO HAVE THE DROP ON A STRANGER.

BUT TARZAN MADE A SIGN OF PEACE, THEN DEMANDED: "WHY ARE YOU HERE? THESE ARE ISHTAK'S LANDS."

"THESE LANDS ARE OURS. WE BOUGHT THEM OF ISHTAK AND PAID HIM WELL. SEE------" HE DREW FORTH A PARCHMENT. "THIS IS THE CONTRACT, SEALED BY ISHTAK'S HANDPRINT."

"GIVE IT TO ME," TARZAN COMMANDED. SOMETHING IN THE PATRI- ARCH'S SIMPLE HEART MOVED HIM TO TRUST THE STATELY STRANGER.

SO HE GAVE THE PARCHMENT INTO THE HANDS OF TARZAN, WHO TURNED AND RACED AWAY.

"YOU FOOL! IT'S A TRICK!" CRIED PIET DE VILLIERS, AND RAISED HIS MUSKET TO BRING DOWN THE SPEEDING APE-MAN. *NEXT WEEK:* **TARZAN'S HAZARD**

Tarzan
by Edgar Rice Burroughs

TARZAN'S HAZARD

WITH QUICK DECISION JAN VAN BOEREN, STRUCK DOWN THE MUSKET AIMED AT TARZAN'S BACK.

"YOU ARE A GOOD MAN, JAN," SAID ANOTHER; "BUT YOU WERE A FOOL TO GIVE THE DOCUMENT TO THE STRANGER."

"BUT WE MUST RECOVER THE CONTRACT" CRIED PIET DE VILLIERS; "IT IS OUR PROOF THAT ISHTAK SOLD US THESE LANDS."

OLD JAN SHOOK HIS HEAD. "IN HIM WAS NO DECEIT. HE WAS AS NATURAL AS A BEAST."

MEANWHILE TARZAN TRAVERSED THE PLAIN, WONDERING IF THE PIONEERS WERE JUST IN THEIR CLAIMS.

OFTEN, HE KNEW, EVEN HONEST WHITE MEN LOST THEIR SENSE OF FAIRNESS, IN DEALING WITH PRIMITIVE RACES.

HE MUST FIND ISHTAK AND EXTRACT FROM HIM THE ANSWER TO THIS DISTURBING PUZZLE.

TRAVELING SILENTLY THROUGH THE TREES, HE FOUND THE BLACKS ENCAMPED IN A JUNGLE GLADE.

WHEN THEY SLEPT, HE DROPPED DOWN AMONG THEM, WATCHFUL OF THE SENTRIES WHO FRINGED THE BIVOUAC.

THESE WERE HIS SAVAGE AND TREACHEROUS FOES, HUNGRY FOR HIS BLOOD.

TO REMOVE ISHTAK FROM HIS WARRIOR HORDE WAS A TASK OF A HUNDRED HAZARDS.

BUT TARZAN CREPT STEADILY FORWARD, THOUGH EVERY STEP, PERHAPS, WAS A STEP TOWARD DEATH!

NEXT WEEK: **TARZAN'S GRAVE ERROR**

Tarzan
by Edgar Rice Burroughs

TARZAN'S GRAVE ERROR

WITH DELICATE, JUNGLE-TRAINED SKILL, TARZAN STEPPED NOISELESSLY AMONG THE WARRIORS. WHEN HE REACHED ISHTAK—

—HE TOUCHED HIS KNIFE TO THE CHIEF AND SAID: "TARZAN HAS COME FOR YOU." ONE SOUND, AND YOU DIE!"

WARILY HE LIFTED THE TERRIFIED MAN TO A SHOULDER AND SLIPPED FROM THE CIRCLE OF WARRIORS.

IN THE CLEAR, HE SPRANG TREEWARD, BORE HIS BURDEN INTO THE FOREST, AND WAITED UNTIL DAYBREAK.

THEN HE EXAMINED THE SETTLER'S CONTRACT AND FOUND THAT ISHTAK'S HANDPRINT SIGNATURE WAS GENUINE.

"THEY TRICKED ME," ISHTAK WAILED, "I DID NOT KNOW THE WRITING GAVE LANDS TO THE WHITES."

"THEN HOW DO YOU KNOW IT NOW?" TARZAN DEMANDED; "I HAVE NOT SAID WHAT WAS IN THE WRITING. ISHTAK, YOU LIE!"

THE CHIEF TREMBLED AS TARZAN CONTINUED; "THE WHITE MEN PAID YOU—AXES FOR WARRIORS—CLOTH FOR WOMEN."

THE APE-MAN SCOWLED: "YOU LURED THE SETTLERS HERE TO RAID THEM; YOU TRIED TO DECEIVE ME INTO AIDING YOU."

QUAILING WITH FEAR, ISHTAK CONFESSED. "SPARE ME," HE PLEADED, "AND I SHALL LEAVE THEM IN PEACE."

"YOU DESERVE DEATH," THE JUNGLE LORD ANSWERED; "BUT I SHALL GRANT YOU MERCY." THEN HE LOWERED ISHTAK AND SET HIM FREE, AND THAT WAS ONE OF THE GRAVEST ERRORS TARZAN EVER MADE!

NEXT WEEK:
THE LONE SCOUT

Tarzan
by Edgar Rice Burroughs

Copr. 1937, Edgar Rice Burroughs, Inc.—Tm. Reg. U.S. Pat.
Off. Produced by Famous Books and Plays. Distributed by
UNITED FEATURE SYNDICATE, Inc.

THE LONE SCOUT

TARZAN BELIEVED ISHTAK'S VOW TO LEAVE THE WHITES IN PEACE, FOR FEW MEN DARED DEFY THE MIGHTY JUNGLE LORD.

BUT AS THE ROGUISH CHIEF FLED BACK TO HIS CAMP, HIS MIND WAS BUSY WITH TREACHEROUS PLANS.

NOW TARZAN RETURNED TO THE TRAIN OF PIONEERS WHO HAILED HIM AS A FRIEND.

JAN VAN BOEREN SHOOK HIS HEAD. "WE ARE A JUST AND STUBBORN PEOPLE. WHAT IS RIGHTLY OURS, WE SHALL HAVE."

"THESE LANDS ARE YOURS," HE SAID; "BUT I ADVISE YOU TO GO BACK. HERE YOU TEMPT THE SAVAGES TO PREY UPON YOU."

TARZAN ADMIRED THIS HIGH RESOLUTION. "THEN YOU MAY COUNT ON MY AID," HE SAID SIMPLY.

THAT NIGHT SETTLERS SLEPT IN PEACE. BEING HONORABLE THEMSELVES THEY TRUSTED ISHTAK'S PROMISE.

BUT TARZAN WAS UNSATISFIED WITH THE SLENDER PRECAUTIONS THEY TOOK.

IN THIS WILD COUNTRY, HE KNEW, NOTHING WAS CERTAIN; INFINITE VIGILANCE WAS THE PRICE OF SAFETY.

HOGARTH—

SO, ALONE HE ROAMED THE VELDT, SCOUTING FOR DANGER, SNIFFING THE AIR, LISTENING INTENTLY.

PRESENTLY HIS JUNGLE-TAUGHT NOSTRILS CAUGHT THE SCENT OF MEN—BLACK MEN. AND HE PERCEIVED DARK FORMS MOVING STEALTHILY ACROSS THE PLAIN IN THE GHOSTLY LIGHT OF THE MOON!—*NEXT WEEK-ATTACK!*

Tarzan

by Edgar Rice Burroughs

TARZAN RECOGNIZED THOSE DARK, STEALTHY FORMS AS ISHTAK'S HORDE, BENT ON A MURDEROUS RAID.

THE APE-MAN WHIRLED, SWIFT AS THE WIND, AND RACED BACK TO SOUND THE ALARM.

AS HE DASHED THROUGH THE THIN SENTRY LINE, HE CRIED: "THE SAVAGES ARE COMING. CLEAR FOR ACTION!"

THE OXEN WERE INSPANNED AND THE BIG COVERED WAGONS CREAKED AND RUMBLED INTO A HOLLOW SQUARE.

QUICKLY, QUIETLY, THE TREK LEADERS PREPARED FOR A DESPERATE DO-OR-DIE DEFENSE.

BUSHES WERE CHOPPED DOWN AND CRAMMED BENEATH THE WAGONS TO BAR THE SAVAGES FROM THE CENTRAL "LAAGER!"

WOMEN AND CHILDREN, TOO, GAVE AID, WITH NEVER A SIGN OF FEAR, FOR THEIRS WERE THE HEARTS OF TRUE PIONEERS.

WHEN ALL WAS IN READINESS, THESE PIOUS FOLK OFFERED UP A FERVENT, THOUGH SILENT PRAYER--AND WAITED.

NOW ISHTAK, SEEING THAT HIS VICTIMS WERE FOREWARNED, COMMANDED A FIERCE, RUSHING ASSAULT.

ARROWS WHIRRED, SINGING A MOURNFUL SONG OF DEATH.

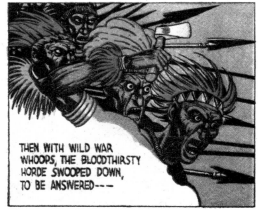

THEN WITH WILD WAR WHOOPS, THE BLOODTHIRSTY HORDE SWOOPED DOWN, TO BE ANSWERED---

HOGARTH—

—BY THE CRACK AND RATTLE OF MUSKETRY, THE BATTLE WAS ON! NEXT WEEK: TARZAN'S DARING

357-1-9-38

Tarzan

by EDGAR RICE BURROUGHS

Copr. 1938 Edgar Rice Burroughs, Inc.—Tm. Reg. U. S. Pat. Off. Produced by Foreign Works and Plans. Distributed by UNITED FEATURE SYNDICATE, Inc.

TARZAN'S DARING

INSTEAD OF STEMMING THE ATTACK, THE BURST OF GUNFIRE STIRRED THE SAVAGES TO RECKLESS FURY.

ON THEY SWEPT, IN WILD ARRAY, AND IN THE HEART OF EACH WAS A YEARNING TO KILL TARZAN, FOR-----

-----ISHTAK, KNOWING THE APE-MAN'S VALUE TO THE WHITES, HAD SET A PRICE UPON HIS HEAD.

IN TRUTH TARZAN'S NATURAL LEADERSHIP QUICKLY BROUGHT HIM TO THE FORE AMONG THE DEFENDERS

HE HURRIED FROM POINT TO POINT IN THE "LAAGER," DIRECTING THE DESPERATE RESISTANCE.

THE MUSKETEERS STUCK GRIMLY TO THE BARRICADES, KNOWING THAT DEFEAT MEANT MASSACRE.

WHEN ONE WAS WOUNDED, SOME VALIANT WOMAN TOOK UP HIS ABANDONED MUSKET.

BUT MORE EFFECTIVE THAN ANY FIREARM WAS TARZAN'S PRIMITIVE BOW. EVERY ARROW FOUND ITS MARK.

BUT PRESENTLY, WHEN HIS QUIVER WAS EMPTY, HE VAULTED UP BETWEEN TWO WAGONS.

"BUT WHERE?" "THERE IS ONLY ONE PLACE," THE APE-MAN REPLIED, LAUGHINGLY--"FROM THE ENEMY!"

"WHERE DO YOU GO?" CRIED JAN VAN BOEREN. "TO GET MORE ARROWS," TARZAN ANSWERED.

HOGARTH—

THEN TARZAN LEAPED DOWN OUTSIDE THE "LAAGER"-----AND WAS GONE!

NEXT WEEK: **THE FLAMING BARRICADE**

358-1-16-38

Tarzan
by EDGAR RICE BURROUGHS

THE FLAMING BARRICADE

TARZAN NEEDED ARROWS. THEY COULD BE HAD ONLY FROM THE ENEMY. SO HE CREPT OUT AMONG THEM.

WHEN HE CAME UPON A SLINKING WARRIOR, THE APE-MAN SET UPON HIM, AND SEIZED HIS QUIVER.

THEN ANOTHER, AND ANOTHER, UNTIL HE HAD A FULL SUPPLY OF SHAFTS.

RETURNING TO THE LAAGER, HE RESUMED HIS DEADLY ARCHERY.

TIME AND AGAIN THE ASSAULTS OF THE SAVAGES WERE REPULSED, AS THEY RESORTED TO STEALTHY APPROACH.

ONCE A BAND OF WARRIORS PENETRATED A SPARSELY MANNED SECTION OF THE BARRICADE.

BUT TARZAN RUSHED A FORCE INTO THE BREECH AND DEALT SWIFTLY WITH THE INVADERS.

THEN THE APE-MAN SAW A PARTY OF SAVAGES APPROACHING THE LAAGER WITH BLAZING FIREBRANDS.

HE SUMMONED A DETACHMENT OF MUSKETEERS TO BLOCK THIS NEW PERIL.

THOUGH THE WARRIORS WEAVED AND DODGED, THEY WERE PICKED OFF ONE BY ONE.

BUT THE LAST, AS HE FELL, FLUNG THE BURNING TORCH UPON A WAGON TOP.

THE CANVAS TOOK FIRE. FLAMES LEAPED TO THE NEXT WAGON. THE WHOLE BARRICADE WAS THREATENED!

HOGARTH—

NEXT WEEK: **INTO THE BREACH**

Tarzan

by EDGAR RICE BURROUGHS

Copr. 1938. Edgar Rice Burroughs Inc.—Tm Reg. U.S.A. Pat.
Off. Produced by Famous Books and Plays. Distributed by
UNITED FEATURE SYNDICATE, Inc.

INTO THE BREACH

FROM THE WARRIOR'S TORCH, THREE WAGONS TOOK FIRE. SOON THE PROTECTIVE BARRICADE WOULD BE DESTROYED.

BUT UNDER TARZAN'S ALERT DIRECTION, THE VEHICLES WERE DRAGGED QUICKLY FROM THE LINE.

THIS MANEUVER, HOWEVER, LEFT A DANGEROUS HOLE IN THE BARRICADE.

QUICK TO PROFIT BY IT, ISHTAK SHOUTED A COMMAND: "THROUGH THE BREACH! HURRY!"

BUT TARZAN HURLED A FORCE INTO THE GAP, TO HOLD IT DOGGEDLY AGAINST THE FIERCE ASSAULT.

AT LAST DAWN CAME, AND THE SAVAGES FLED TO THEIR JUNGLE RETREAT, LEAVING MANY DEAD ON THE FIELD.

"NOW YOU SEE THE DANGER OF THIS COUNTRY," TARZAN SAID TO JAN VAN BOEREN; "WHY NOT GO BACK?"

BUT IN ALL THE COMPANY, ONLY ONE AGREED WITH TARZAN. THAT ONE WAS ANNITJE, VAN BOEREN'S ADOPTED DAUGHTER.

"LET US GO BACK," SHE SOBBED; "THE SAVAGES WILL KILL ME." IT WAS HER HABIT TO THINK ONLY OF HERSELF.

OLD JAN HAD A COUNT TAKEN OF THE DEAD AND WOUNDED THEN STUBBORNLY SHOOK HIS HEAD.

"THIS SOIL IS OURS BY THE BLOOD OF OUR PEOPLE. WE WILL NOT ABANDON IT. WE WILL GO ON."

HOGARTH—

TARZAN NODDED. "THEN MY PATH IS BESIDE YOURS— MY WAY, TOO, LIES FORWARD."

NEXT WEEK: **TARZAN ON PATROL**

360-1-30-38

Tarzan
by Edgar Rice Burroughs

Copr. 1938, Edgar Rice Burroughs, Inc. — Tm. Reg. U. S. Pat. Off. — Predominante in Previous Number and Price Distributed by UNITED FEATURE SYNDICATE, Inc.

TARZAN ON PATROL

WHEN TARZAN VOLUNTEERED TO JOIN THE PIONEERS, ANNITJE'S CAPRICIOUS HEART WAS THRILLED.

ALL THE MAIDENS CAST SHY, ADMIRING GLANCES AT THE HANDSOME JUNGLE LORD, WHO WAS THE HERO OF LAST NIGHT'S BATTLE.

BUT ANNITJE'S BEWITCHING EYES FOLLOWED HIM BOLDLY AS HE STRODE AWAY.

SOON THE OXEN WERE INSPANNED, AND THE CARAVAN PUSHED ON INTO THE UNKNOWN.

FAR IN ADVANCE, TARZAN CAPTAINED A MOUNTED PATROL OF DARING YOUTHS, SCOUTING FOR DANGER.

AT LAST THE TRAIN WAS HALTED, THE LANDS WERE DIVIDED, AND EACH FAMILY SET OUT FOR ITS OWN ISOLATED TRACK.

TARZAN'S SCOUTS WERE DISBANDED, FOR EVERY HAND WAS NEEDED IN THE WORK OF SETTLEMENT.

BUT TARZAN CONTINUED THE PATROL, RIDING THE VELDT ALONE, EVER ALERT FOR SIGNS OF SAVAGE RAIDERS.

THROUGHOUT THE NEW LAND, THE COLONISTS WERE BUSY RAISING HOMES, BUILDING KRAALS FOR THE LIVESTOCK.

ALL BELIEVED THE SAVAGE FOES HAD HAD THEIR LESSON AND WOULD LEAVE THEM IN PEACE.

SUCH WAS ISHTAK'S PLAN, TO LURE THEM INTO A SENSE OF SECURITY---THEN STRIKE!

"EVEN TARZAN CANNOT BALK US," HE ASSERTED "WHEN WE HURL A WAR PARTY AGAINST A LONE FARMHOUSE!"
NEXT WEEK: **ANNITJE THE FLIRT**

HOGARTH

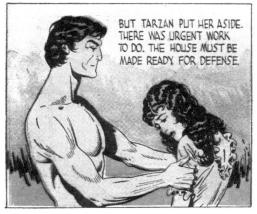

Tarzan

by EDGAR RICE BURROUGHS

BESIEGED

WITH WILD WAR WHOOPS, THE SAVAGES HURLED THEMSELVES FURIOUSLY AGAINST THE FARMHOUSE, WHILE --------

—INSIDE, TARZAN AND THE VAN BOEREN FAMILY TOOK UP THE DESPERATE DEFENSE. AS THE MEN POURED DEADLY VOLLEYS INTO THE HOWLING HORDE, THREE BRAVE WOMEN STOOD BY, LOADING THE MUSKETS.

ONLY ANNITJE, SCREAMING HYSTERICALLY, WAS USELESS.

SOON THE ASSAILANTS HACKED THEIR WAY THROUGH THE CENTER DOOR.

WITH CRIES OF TRIUMPH, A BAND OF WARRIORS PLUNGED INTO THE GAP.

BUT THE MIGHTY APE-MAN AND STOUT OLD JAN BATTERED THEM DOWN.

DISCOURAGED AT LAST BY THEIR HEAVY LOSSES, THE SAVAGES RETIRED IN DISORDER.

THE EYES OF JAN VAN BOEREN LIGHTED WITH JOY. "THEY ARE GONE! WE ARE SAVED!"

BUT WHEN THE NEW DAY ROLLED ACROSS THE VELDT, IT REVEALED THE SAVAGE WARRIORS SURROUNDING THE HOMESTEAD.

"WE ARE BESIEGED," TARZAN EXPLAINED. "THEY WILL SEND FOR REINFORCEMENTS AND RENEW THE ATTACK TONIGHT."

NEXT WEEK: HERO OF THE VELDT

HOGARTH—

OLD JAN NODDED. "WE ARE TRAPPED. WE SHALL DIE — BUT WE WILL DIE FIGHTING!"

Tarzan
by EDGAR RICE BURROUGHS

HERO OF
THE VELDT

BESIEGED BY THE SAVAGE HORDE, TARZAN AND THE VAN BOERENS KNEW THAT THE NIGHT WOULD BRING A FRESH ATTACK.

SUDDENLY THE WATCHFUL APE-MAN PERCEIVED A COMMOTION AMONG THE SAVAGES. THEN HE SAW THE CAUSE.

A LONE HORSEMAN RODE OUT, TRYING TO PENETRATE THE CIRCLE OF WARRIORS. HE WAS STEFANUS VAN BOEREN.

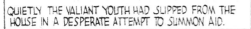

QUIETLY THE VALIANT YOUTH HAD SLIPPED FROM THE HOUSE IN A DESPERATE ATTEMPT TO SUMMON AID.

BUT HIS BRAVE SALLY WAS IN VAIN. A VOLLEY OF ARROWS BROUGHT DOWN HORSE AND RIDER!

TARZAN BOWED IN SILENT SALUTE TO THIS BOY HERO OF THE VELDT. OLD JAN BIT HIS LIPS TO HIDE HIS GRIEF.

AND DOWN THE STOIC CHEEK OF MOTHER VAN BOEREN TRICKLED A TEAR, BUT SHE GAVE NO OTHER SIGN OF THE ACHE IN HER HEART.

ONLY ANNITJE WEPT OPENLY— NOT FOR STEFANUS, BUT BECAUSE HIS DEATH MIGHT BE A SHADOW OF HER OWN IMPENDING FATE.

NOW SUDDENLY, FROM AFAR, CAME A THUNDERING ROAR, AND ON THE HORIZON LOOMED A HERD OF STAMPEDING WILDEBEEST.

THE SAVAGES BROKE ONE SEGMENT OF THEIR CIRCLE AND SCURRIED TO ESCAPE THOSE DEADLY HOOFS. THEN TARZAN SAW HIS CHANCE TO ACCOMPLISH THE PURPOSE FOR WHICH STEFANUS HAD DIED.

HE LEAPED THROUGH THE DOORWAY AND RACED STRAIGHT TOWARD THE MAD STAMPEDING HERD!
NEXT WEEK: **SHADOW OF DOOM!**

Tarzan and the Boers, Part I   53

Tarzan

by EDGAR RICE BURROUGHS

A RACE WITH DEATH

BELIEVING VICTORY WAS CERTAIN, THE HOWLING SAVAGES ATTACKED WITH RECKLESS FURY.

THE VAN BOERENS KNEW THEY COULD NOT HOLD OUT LONG, FOR THEIR AMMUNITION WAS ALMOST EXHAUSTED.

MEANWHILE, TARZAN RACED TO FAR-FLUNG FARMS, RAISING AN ARMED FORCE TO RELIEVE THE BESIEGED FAMILY.

THEN HE DASHED ACROSS THE VELDT AT THE HEAD OF A MOUNTED TROOP OF PIONEERS. BUT IT SEEMED THEY WOULD SURELY LOSE THEIR WILD RACE WITH DEATH.

ALREADY THE ATTACKERS WERE HACKING AT THE DOORS, AND THE DEFENDERS ABANDONED HOPE.

BUT THE STOUT-HEARTED VAN BOEREN MEN EXPECTED TO DIE FIGHTING.

AND NOW MOTHER VAN BOEREN CALLED HER DAUGHTERS TO HER AS SHE PLACED FOUR BULLETS ON A TABLE. "THESE," SHE SAID, "ARE FOR US; IT IS BETTER TO DIE NOW THAN SUFFER TORTURE AT THE HANDS OF THE SAVAGES."

"MUST WE KILL OURSELVES," ANNITJE MOANED. "NO," THE OTHER REPLIED; I SHALL TAKE THE SIN UPON MYSELF—IF SIN IT BE."

THEN THE ELDEST DAUGHTER STEPPED FORWARD AND SAID IN CALM, FIRM TONES; "I AM READY, MOTHER."

"HEAVEN HAVE MERCY ON HER SOUL—AND MINE," SHE BREATHED, AND RAISED THE MUSKET TO FIRE!

NEXT WEEK: MYSTERY AND ALARM

HOGARTH—

MYSTERY AND ALARM

"IT IS BETTER TO DIE THAN FALL INTO THE HANDS OF THE SAVAGES," BREATHED MOTHER VAN BOEREN AND SO, AS THE WARRIORS HACKED AT THE DOOR, SHE STEELED HERSELF TO KILL HER BELOVED DAUGHTERS.

BUT SUDDENLY FROM OUTSIDE CAME EXCITED SHOUTS, THEN GUNFIRE AND THE THUNDER OF RACING HOOFS

A WILD, HAPPY CRY BURST FROM OLD JAN'S THROAT: "TARZAN! HE COMES! WE ARE SAVED!

TRUE, LIKE A CYCLONE, THE APE-MAN'S TROOP SWEPT OUT OF THE WEST TO ROUT THE SAVAGE RAIDERS

WHEN TARZAN HURRIED TO THE HOUSE, ANNITJE BUBBLED WITH JOY AND FLUNG HER ARMS AROUND HIM.

THE AUSTERE FRONTIERSMEN WERE SCANDALIZED AND MOTHER VAN BOEREN SENT HER STERNLY AWAY.

THE MUSKETEERS RODE FORTH TO SEE WHERE ELSE THEY WERE NEEDED. THEY FOUND ANOTHER HOMESTEAD BESIEGED.

THEIR MUSKETS SPOKE— AND WERE ANSWERED BY RIFLE FIRE! BUT THE BLACKS WERE DRIVEN AWAY.

ON THE BATTLEFIELD THE FUGITIVES LEFT THREE MODERN RIFLES. TARZAN INSPECTED THEM WITH PUZZLED ALARM.

WHENCE CAME THESE POWERFUL WEAPONS? COULD THE SAVAGES OBTAIN A FULL SUPPLY OF THEM? IF THEY COULD, THEN THE DOOM OF TARZAN AND THE PIONEERS WAS SEALED! *NEXT WEEK:* THE PIONEER FORTRESS

HOGARTH

347-3-20-38

Tarzan
by EDGAR RICE BURROUGHS

THE PIONEER FORTRESS

TARZAN'S TROOPERS FOUND TWO MORE HOMESTEADS LOOTED, AND THE DWELLERS MASSACRED BY HATCHET AND GUN.

"WITH RIFLES, THE SAVAGE HORDE WILL WIPE US OUT," GROWLED ONE OF THE BAND.

"WE MUST ATTACK THEM IN THEIR MOUNTAIN LAIR BEFORE THEY GET MORE GUNS," SAID ANOTHER

"BUT FIRST," TARZAN URGED; "WE MUST BUILD A FORTIFIED TOWN AS A REFUGE FOR THE WOMEN AND CHILDREN."

AND SO THE WORD WENT OUT. ONCE MORE THE OXEN WERE INSPANNED; ONCE MORE THE GREAT WAGONS RUMBLED----- AND THE UPROOTED SETTLERS CONVERGED ON THE PLACE APPOINTED FOR THE TOWN.

GREAT TIMBERS WERE BROUGHT FROM THE DISTANT FOREST; STONES WERE GATHERED FROM THE PLAIN.

SOON STOUT LITTLE COTTAGES BEGAN TO RISE IN THE WILDERNESS.

AROUND THEM, TARZAN DIRECTED CONSTRUCTION OF WALLS AND RAMPARTS.

EVERY NIGHT ISHTAK'S SPIES CREPT THROUGH THE TALL GRASS TO VIEW THE WORK OF THEIR FOES.

AND ALWAYS THEY REPORTED TO THEIR CHIEF: "THE WHITE MEN'S STOCKADE GROWS STRONGER!"

HOGARTH—

ISHTAK LAUGHED. "LET THEM BUILD TO THE SKIES. WHEN WE GET MORE GUNS, THEIR TOWN WILL BE THEIR TOMB!" NEXT WEEK: **LOVE INTO HATE**

Tarzan and the Boers, Part I   57

Tarzan

by EDGAR RICE BURROUGHS

LOVE INTO HATE

AS TARZAN DIRECTED THE BUILDING OF THE FORTIFIED TOWN, ONE MAN RAISED HIS VOICE AGAINST HIM.

HE WAS HENRIK SMIT, WHO SAID: "WHY DO WE ALLOW THIS OUTLANDER TO RULE US? ARE WE TOO WEAK TO ORDER OUR OWN AFFAIRS?"

"HE IS WISE AND JUST," ANSWERED JAN VAN BOEREN: "AND HE IS OUR SALVATION AGAINST THE SAVAGES."

"HE MAY BE IN LEAGUE WITH THEM," SMIT INSISTED; "---PREPARING TO BETRAY US."

THE PIONEERS SCOFFED, AND TARZAN WONDERED WHY THIS MAN WAS HIS ENEMY.

DESPITE THE FELLOW'S SLURS, THE APE-MAN WAS A HERO, AND THE MAIDENS STOLE SHY GLANCES AT HIM.

BUT ANNITJE'S PERSISTENT FLIRTATION WAS BOLD AND SHAMELESS.

OLD LADIES WAGGED THEIR HEADS AND SAID: "IT IS PLAIN THAT SHE IS NOT OF OUR KIND."

TRUE, ANNITJE WAS OF STRANGE ORIGIN. AS A CHILD SHE WAS FOUND IN THE VELDT AFTER THE MASSACRE OF HER UNIDENTIFIED PARENTS.

THE VAN BOEREN'S ADOPTED HER, AND SHE GREW INTO A VAIN, HIGH-TEMPERED GIRL, AN ALIEN TO THESE SIMPLE FOLK.

TARZAN WAS COOL TO HER BRAZEN ADVANCES, AND ANNITJE SMARTED UNDER THIS BLOW TO HER VANITY.

THUS HER FANCY FOR HIM TURNED TO HATRED, AND SHE VOWED REVENGE.

NEXT WEEK:

THE TRAITOR

HOGARTH—

Tarzan
by EDGAR RICE BURROUGHS

THE TRAITOR

WHEN TARZAN IGNORED HER, THE FURIOUS ANNITJE TURNED TO HENRIK SMIT WHO HAD LONG SOUGHT HER FAVOR.

SHE KNEW HE HATED TARZAN, AND THROUGH HIM SHE MIGHT CONTRIVE REVENGE ON THE MAN WHO SPURNED HER.

"DON'T BOTHER ABOUT HIM," SMIT GRINNED SLYLY. "TARZAN HAS NOT LONG TO LIVE." HE WOULD NOT SAY MORE.

AS STOREKEEPER, SMIT LEFT NEXT DAY FOR THE DISTANT CITY TO TRADE WOOL FOR SUPPLIES--- CHIEFLY AMMUNITION.

TARZAN WAS PUZZLED WHEN SMIT REFUSED AN ARMED ESCORT TO PROTECT HIM FROM THE SAVAGES.

ON THE EVENING OF SMIT'S RETURN, THE APE-MAN MET ANNITJE TRIPPING JAUNTILY FROM HIS STORE.

INSTEAD OF PASSING HIM BY, SHE GAILY FLAUNTED A GOLDEN BRACELET BEFORE HIS EYES.

"YOU SEE, SOMEONE CARES FOR ME," SHE TAUNTED, THEN SKIPPED AWAY.

TARZAN FROWNED. WHERE HAD HE SEEN SUCH A BRACELET BEFORE?---- AH YES, IN THE CAMP OF THE SAVAGE FOE!

INTO THE STORE HE DASHED. "I KNOW NOW, SMIT, WHY YOU TAKE NO COMRADES TO MARKET!"

THE STOREKEEPER GAPED AS TARZAN CONTINUED: "YOU MEET OUR ENEMIES AND GIVE THEM GUNS FOR GOLD!"

HOGARTH—
SMIT WENT WHITE. HIS TREACHERY WAS DISCOVERED. THE DISCOVERER MUST DIE----NOW!
NEXT WEEK- ON THE WARPATH

Tarzan and the Boers, Part I   59

370-4-10-38

Tarzan

by Edgar Rice Burroughs

Copr. 1938 Edgar Rice Burroughs Inc—Reg. U.S. Pat. Off. Printed in Foreign. Single and Public Distribution by UNITED FEATURE SYNDICATE, Inc

ON THE WARPATH

ONE THOUGHT GRIPPED SMIT'S MIND— TO KILL TARZAN, WHO HAD DISCOVERED HIS SALE OF GUNS TO THE FOE. BUT AS HIS HAND FUMBLED FOR THE REVOLVER, TARZAN SPRANG.

CLEARING THE COUNTER IN A FLYING LEAP, THE APE-MAN POUNCED UPON THE GREEDY STOREKEEPER.

HE WRENCHED THE GUN AWAY AND TOSSED IT ASIDE; THEN HIS FINGERS TIGHTENED ON THE SCOUNDREL'S THROAT.

"SMIT'S TREACHERY HAD STIRRED THE JUNGLE LORD TO FURY. "YOU SCURVY JACKAL," HE GROWLED.

HE MIGHT HAVE THROTTLED THE FELLOW HAD HE NOT BEEN STARTLED BY A SHOT IN THE DISTANCE.

IT WAS THE ALARM GUN FROM THE WATCHTOWER FOLLOWED BY A VOLLEY OF SHOTS.

TARZAN FLUNG SMIT ASIDE AND DASHED OUT; THERE WOULD BE TIME LATER TO DEAL WITH THE TRAITOR.

SOON FROM A TOWER, TARZAN BEHELD A SWARM OF WARRIORS. ISHTAK'S HORDE WAS ON THE WARPATH!

FROM THEIR NIGHT-SHROUDED RANKS A HUNDRED RIFLES BLAZED---RIFLES THAT SMIT HAD SOLD THEM.

FRENZIED WARWHOOPS, CRIES FOR BLOOD, BURST FROM A THOUSAND SAVAGE THROATS.

HOGARTH—

AND WITHIN THE WALLS RANG THE BATTLECRY OF THE PIONEERS: "TO ARMS! TO ARMS! THEIR LIVES OR OURS!"
NEXT WEEK: BATTLE

Tarzan

by EDGAR RICE BURROUGHS

Copr. 1938 Edgar Rice Burroughs, Inc.—Trade Reg. U. S. Pat.
Off. Produced by Famous Books and Plays. Distributed by
UNITED FEATURE SYNDICATE, Inc.

BATTLE

371-4-17-38

LIKE A CONSUMING PRAIRIE FIRE THE SAVAGE HORDE SWEPT ACROSS THE VELDT———

———WHILE WITHIN THE WALLS THE THIN BAND OF PIONEERS RALLIED TO THE DEFENSE.

SOME TOOK UP STATIONS ON THE RAISED PLATFORMS; OTHERS FIRED THROUGH THE LOOPHOLES IN THE WALLS.

TARZAN SEEMED EVERYWHERE AT ONCE, DISPOSING HIS MEAGER FORCES TO BEST ADVANTAGE.

HE URGED THE WOMEN TO SEEK SHELTER IN AN INNER SECTION OF THE TOWN, BUT ONE ANSWERED FOR ALL: "WE HAVE SHARED THE LIVES OF OUR MENFOLK——WE SHALL STAND BY THEM IN DEATH!"

MANY OF THEM TOOK UP ARMS; OTHERS SERVED AS LOADERS; NONE WAS IDLE.

THOUGH THE FIRE OF THE PIONEERS TOOK HEAVY TOLL, THE SAVAGES SURGED ONWARD IN STORMY WAVES.

TARZAN SMILED, FOR THE BULLETS AND ARROWS OF THE FOE SPLINTERED AND SPLASHED HARMLESSLY AGAINST HIS WALL.

SOON THE RANKS OF THE SAVAGES DIVIDED TO ATTACK ON ALL SIDES AND SPLIT THE DEFENDERS' FORCES!

THEN THE APE-MAN WAS DISMAYED TO SEE THAT THEY CARRIED A SCORE OF SCALING LADDERS.

HOGARTH—

IF THEY SURMOUNTED THE WALLS ALL WAS LOST——MASSACRE WAS INEVITABLE!——NEXT WEEK——VILLAINY

Tarzan and the Boers, Part I   61

Tarzan
by EDGAR RICE BURROUGHS

VILLAINY

"CENTER YOUR FIRE ON THE MEN WITH THE SCALING LADDERS," TARZAN DIRECTED.

FLASHING VOLLEYS RIPPED THE RANKS OF THE SAVAGES, AND THEY FELL BACK.

THREE TIMES THE FOE SURGED FORWARD AND WAS THRICE REPULSED.

"WE'VE PLENTY OF POWDER; WE CAN HOLD THEM OFF," JAN VAN BOEREN CRIED CHEERILY.

NOW THE WOMEN HURRIED TO SMIT'S STORE FOR FRESH SUPPLIES OF POWDER, SHOT, AND CARTRIDGES.

BUT WHEN THE NEW AMMUNITION WAS LOADED INTO MUSKET AND RIFLE, IT FAILED TO FIRE.

"THE DEALER CHEATED ME," SMIT LIED, TO COVER THE FACT THAT HE HAD DELIBERATELY SPOILED THE POWDER.

LATER HE CONFIDED TO ANNITJE; "THE SAVAGES PROMISED ME MUCH GOLD IF THEY TAKE THE TOWN TONIGHT."

AT FIRST THE GIRL WAS SHOCKED BY HIS TREACHERY, BUT HER VANITY WAS DAZZLED BY THE PROSPECT OF RICHES.

"THEN WE CAN GO TO THE CITY AND LIVE IN LUXURY," SHE COOED; "YOU ARE WONDERFUL, HENRIK."

NOW WITHOUT AMMUNITION, THE DEFENDERS WERE HELPLESS TO STEM THE SAVAGE TIDE.

HOGARTH—

WITH SHRIEKS OF TRIUMPH THE WARRIORS SET THE LADDERS AGAINST THE WALL AND CLAMBERED UP! NEXT WEEK: **TO THE RAMPARTS**

Tarzan

373-5-1-38

by Edgar Rice Burroughs

Copr. 1938 Edgar Rice Burroughs, Inc.—The Reg. U.S. Pat.
Off. Produced by Famous Books and Plays. Distributed by
UNITED FEATURE SYNDICATE, Inc.

TO THE
RAMPARTS

LIKE FRENZIED HORNETS THE SAVAGES
SWARMED UP THE LONG SCALING LADDERS.

SINCE THE DEFENDERS HAD EXHAUSTED
THEIR AMMUNITION, THE WARRIORS
FORESAW SWIFT VICTORY.

"TO THE WALLS!" TARZAN SHOUTED:
"EVERY MAN TO THE WALLS!"

THE COLONISTS
MOUNTED THE
RAMPARTS AND
SWUNG THEIR
GUNS AS CLUBS.
HEADS CRACKED.

BUT THE WARRIORS
REPLIED WITH THRUSTING SPEARS
AND SLASHING HATCHETS IN HAND-
TO-HAND CONFLICT.

THEN CAME THE BRAVE PIONEER
WOMEN WITH BOILING WATER
TO DASH UPON THE CLIMBERS.

THIS GAVE TARZAN AN IDEA. "GO
FETCH ROPE, AND THE HOOKS OF
YOUR COOKING POTS," HE DIRECTED.

WITH THESE
THE DEFENDERS
GRAPPLED THE
LADDERS.

SOME WERE TOPPLED OVER; A FEW WERE DRAWN OUT
OF REACH. OTHERS ROSE UP IN THEIR PLACES.

BUT UNDER TARZAN'S LEADERSHIP
THE VALIANT SETTLERS WERE
HOLDING THEIR OWN.

PRESENTLY, SMIT, THE TRAITOR, VENTURED
FORTH AND SAW THAT THE BATTLE WAS IN THE BALANCE.

"BUT I CAN GIVE THE VICTORY TO THE SAVAGES," HE MUTTERED
DARKLY." *NEXT WEEK*: THE ENEMY WITHIN

HOGARTH—

Tarzan
by EDGAR RICE BURROUGHS

THE ENEMY WITHIN

SMIT, THE TRAITOR, OBSERVED THAT ALL HIS COMPATRIOTS WERE FIGHTING FURIOUSLY ON THE WALLS.

SO HE CREPT FURTIVELY TO THE UNGUARDED GATES AND OPENED THE SMALL DOOR.

SOFTLY HE CALLED THE PASSWORD THAT IDENTIFIED HIM TO THE SAVAGES.

ISHTAK, THE CHIEF, HEARD HIM AND CAME RUNNING WITH A DETACHMENT OF WARRIORS

"YOU COME IN TIME," BREATHED ISHTAK; "WE ARE IN NEED OF AMMUNITION." SMIT LED THEM SECRETLY TO HIS STORE.

"I GAVE BAD AMMUNITION TO WHITE MEN; SAVED GOOD FOR YOU," HE EXPLAINED; "FOR THIS YOU MUST PAY MUCH GOLD."

"BWANA SMIT SMART MAN," THE BLACK SNARLED; "ISHTAK SMART, TOO. ISHTAK TAKE EVERYTHING, PAY NOTHING."

SMIT RESISTED. ISHTAK CLEFT HIS SKULL WITH A HAND-AXE.

ANNITJE RAN. A WARRIOR SHOT HER DOWN.

THUS DID THESE TWO PAY WITH THEIR LIVES FOR THEIR TREACHERY AND GREED.

THEN ISHTAK SENT A MESSENGER TO THROW WIDE THE BIG GATES AND ADMIT THE SAVAGE HORDE.

HOGARTH—

FIVE SCORE WARRIORS SLIPPED INTO THE WALLED TOWN, BEFORE-----

NEXT WEEK: THE FLYING SQUADRON

----TARZAN DISCOVERED THEM. NOW THE DEFENDERS WERE TRAPPED BETWEEN TWO JAWS OF THE MONSTROUS FOE!

375-5-15-38

Tarzan
by EDGAR RICE BURROUGHS

THE FLYING SQUADRON

A HUNDRED WARRIORS HAD PENETRATED THE WALLS BEFORE TARZAN DISCOVERED THEM.

QUICKLY HE GATHERED A FLYING SQUADRON FOR A DESPERATE ATTEMPT TO STEM THE SAVAGE TIDE.

THE APE-MAN HIMSELF WAS THE THIN EDGE OF THE WEDGE THAT BIT INTO THE WARRIOR RANKS.

LUCKILY THE BLACKS WERE WITHOUT CARTRIDGES-- AND THE PIONEERS------

---PRESSED THEM SO CLOSELY THAT THEY COULD USE NEITHER SPEARS NOR ARROWS EFFECTIVELY.

AT LAST THE ATTACKERS CUT THE LINE, AND RAMMED THE GATES SHUT.

THEN THEY TURNED FULL FORCE UPON THE CONFUSED TRIBESMEN.

SOME WERE SLAIN, BUT MOST OF THEM FLED WITH ISHTAK'S MESSENGER TO THE ARSENAL.

THERE THEY BARRICADED THEMSELVES WITH THE PLENTIFUL SUPPLY OF MUNITIONS, AND OPENED A WITHERING FIRE.

THE PIONEERS WERE FORCED TO WITHDRAW AND LEAVE THE ARSENAL IN THE HANDS OF THE FOE.

HOGARTH—

NEXT WEEK:
SHADOW OF DEFEAT

THEN ISHTAK DECIDED TO MAKE A SALLY, RE-OPEN THE GATES, AND ADMIT HIS WHOLE ARMY. "CHARGE!" HE COMMANDED; AND THE SAVAGES CAME OUT SHOOTING.

Tarzan

by Edgar Rice Burroughs

SHADOW OF DEFEAT

ISHTAK'S COMPANY CAME OUT SHOOTING, DETERMINED TO GAIN THE GATES AND OPEN THEM TO THEIR COMRADES.

THE PIONEERS WANTED TO HURL THEMSELVES AT THE SAVAGES, BUT TARZAN RESTRAINED THEIR SUICIDAL ZEAL.

THEN HE LED A SHAM RETREAT INTO A SIDE STREET, AND ISHTAK BELIEVED THE WAY WAS CLEAR.

BUT TARZAN CIRCLED AHEAD AND STATIONED HIS MEN IN HIDING, WHILE------

-----HE HIMSELF CLIMBED TO THE ROOF OF A LOW BUILDING.

WHEN THE BLACKS SWEPT PAST, THE PIONEERS SET UPON THEM FROM THE REAR.

THE APE-MAN LEAPED DOWN UPON ISHTAK, THE CHIEF.

AND THE TWO FORCES CLASHED IN MORTAL COMBAT.

MEANWHILE, THE FEW DEFENDERS LEFT ON THE WALLS WERE POWERLESS TO STEM THE SAVAGE TIDE.

LIKE DEMONS THEY SWARMED INTO THE TOWN, TO KILL, TO PLUNDER, TO DESTROY.

TARZAN'S FORCE, TOO, WAS ON THE VERGE OF DEFEAT.

AND AS THE APE-MAN STRUGGLED WITH ISHTAK, ONE OF THE SAVAGES JABBED A LOADED RIFLE AGAINST HIM!
NEXT WEEK: CALL OF THE JUNGLE!!!

CALL OF THE JUNGLE

AS THE WARRIOR'S RIFLE JABBED TARZAN'S RIBS, ONE OF THE PIONEERS STRUCK IT DOWN.

THE APE-MAN FOUGHT ON AGAINST THE POWERFUL ISHTAK AND LOCKED HIM AT LAST IN A STEELY GRIP.

WHEN THE INVADERS SAW THEIR CHIEFTAIN VANQUISHED PANIC SEIZED THEM.

NOW, AT TARZAN'S DIRECTION, THE DEFENDERS RACED TO THE STOREHOUSE FOR FRESH MUNITIONS—

—AND LAUNCHED A SMASHING DRIVE. MANY OF THE FOE WERE SLAIN; SOME WERE CAPTURED; THE REST FLED.

ONE OF THE CAPTIVES SNARLED AT THE FALLEN ISHTAK, AND THE PUZZLED TARZAN ASKED HIM WHY.

"I WAS CHIEF," THE MAN SAID; "BUT EVIL ISHTAK OVERTHREW ME AND FORCED US TO WAR WITH THE WHITE MEN."

"I WISH PEACE," HE CONTINUED. "THERE IS LAND ENOUGH FOR ALL." SO A TREATY WAS SIGNED.

AND THE PIONEERS KNELT IN THANKSGIVING FOR VICTORY AND FOR PEACE TO CARVE A NEW DOMAIN FROM THE WILDERNESS.

THEY PLANNED TO HONOR TARZAN, WHOM THEY CALLED HEAVEN-SENT TO SAVE THEM FROM DESTRUCTION.

AND AS HE TRAVELLED HOMEWARD, THE FICKLE HAND OF FATE PREPARED TO THRUST HIM INTO AN AMAZING ADVENTURE.

HOGARTH

THAT NIGHT, HOWEVER, TARZAN SLIPPED AWAY. HIS TASK WAS DONE; THE JUNGLE CALLED AGAIN.
-NEXT WEEK-
THE MYSTERIOUS SKELETONS

Tarzan

by Edgar Rice Burroughs

THE MYSTERIOUS SKELETONS

HOMEWARD BOUND, TARZAN CHANGED HIS COURSE TO EXPLORE NEW TERRITORY. HIS WAS A FREE, QUESTING SPIRIT, EAGER TO UNCOVER THE ENDLESS MYSTERIES SHROUDED BY THE WILDERNESS.

SUDDENLY HE STOPPED, SURPRISED. BEFORE HIM TOWERED A GREAT WALL, EVIDENTLY BUILT BY A HIGHLY CIVILIZED RACE.

TARZAN'S BLOOD QUICKENED. THE WALL WAS A CHALLENGE. HE MUST KNOW WHAT SECRETS LAY BEYOND.

TO COMMON MEN IT WAS A COMPLETE BARRIER; TO THE MIGHTY APE-MAN IT WAS A SMALL OBSTACLE.

BUT ONCE ON THE SUMMIT, HE SAW NOTHING BUT THE SHADOWED JUNGLE.

TARZAN DROPPED DOWN. WARILY HE CREPT THROUGH THE FOREST, FOR ANY TREE MIGHT MASK A FOE.

THERE! WHAT WAS THAT? BONES! HUMAN BONES! OVER YONDER----ANOTHER HUMAN REMNANT!

HOW CAME THESE MEN TO DIE? TARZAN WONDERED. INTRIGUED, HE STOOPED TO INSPECT A MANGLED SKELETON.

THEN HIS SENSITIVE EARS DETECTED THE SWISH AND CRACKLE OF UNDERBRUSH.

HE TURNED TO SEE A GREAT LION CHARGING HIM FURIOUSLY. A MOMENT LATER---

---FROM EVERY QUARTER, A SCORE OF MAMMOTH BEASTS RUSHED AT HIM! NEXT WEEK: AMBUSH-

HOGARTH---

Tarzan

by EDGAR RICE BURROUGHS AMBUSH

TARZAN SPRANG TREEWARD BARELY IN TIME TO ESCAPE THAT MAD RUSH OF LIONS.

PRESENTLY THE FOREST WAS TEEMING WITH BEASTS. NOW THE JUNGLE LORD UNDERSTOOD THOSE GRISLY SKELETONS.

HAD HE NOT BEEN TARZAN THE APE-MAN, HE WOULD HAVE SUFFERED THE SAME FATE.

STILL UNDAUNTED, HE PLUNGED DEEPER INTO THE FOREST, UNTIL HE CAME TO ANOTHER WALL, LIKE THE FIRST.

WHAT WAS THE MEANING OF THE STRANGE DEVICE— TWO WALLS ENCLOSING A PACK OF ENORMOUS LIONS?

EVIDENTLY THIS WAS A BARRIER OF BEASTS, TO BAR INTRUDERS FROM THE MYSTERIOUS LAND BEYOND.

TARZAN SCALED THE NEW WALL AND STARTED DOWN THE OTHER SIDE; BUT BELOW----

--A FANTASTIC WARRIOR CAUGHT SIGHT OF HIM THROUGH A SHEET OF POLISHED METAL THAT MIRRORED THE RAMPART.

THE STARTLED WARRIOR WHIRLED AND DISAPPEARED WITHIN THE WALL, WHERE THE FRONTIER GUARDS HAD QUARTERS.

IN THE DARK RECESSES, HE REPORTED TO HIS CAPTAIN: "A STRANGE BARBARIAN COMES!"

THE GUARDSMEN PUT ON MASKS TO GIVE THEMSELVES A FIERCE APPEARANCE, THEN TOOK UP THEIR MAMMOTH SWORDS.

HOGARTH—

AND AS TARZAN DESCENDED, THEY LAY IN WAIT TO SPRING UPON HIM! NEXT WEEK: CAPTURED

Tarzan
by Edgar Rice Burroughs

CAPTURED

WHEN TARZAN REACHED THE GROUND, THE HIDDEN GUARDSMEN SPRANG OUT AND DRAGGED HIM DOWN.

HE FOUND HIMSELF ENCIRCLED BY AN ASTONISHING BAND OF WARRIORS, WEIRD AND FRIGHTFUL IN THEIR WAR MASKS.

NO LESS AMAZED WERE THE GUARDS, FOR NEVER HAD ANY OUTLANDER SURMOUNTED THE BARRIER OF BEASTS.

IN THEIR FIRST MOMENTS OF BEWILDERMENT, TARZAN MIGHT HAVE RISKED A DASH FOR FREEDOM.

NO! HIS CURIOSITY ABOUT THESE PEOPLE PROMPTED HIM TO REMAIN AMONG THEM. HE WOULD TAKE A CHANCE ON ESCAPING LATER.

THE WARRIORS, TRIUMPHANT, TOOK OFF THEIR MASKS. TARZAN SAW THAT THEIR FACES WERE OF ORIENTAL MOLD.

IN THE DIM PAST, HE KNEW, THE ROVERS OF MANY RACES HAD BEEN SWALLOWED UP BY THE AFRICAN WILDERNESS.

NOW THE GUARDSMEN FORMED A HOLLOW SQUARE AND SIGNALLED THEIR PRISONER TO MARCH

SOON THE JUNGLE FADED, AND THE TRAIL MERGED INTO A HIGHWAY THAT WOUND THROUGH A FRUITFUL LAND.

AND AS FAR AS TARZAN'S EYE COULD SEE, THE WALL RAN ON, ENCLOSING THIS VAST, MYSTERIOUS DOMAIN.

"'TIS WELL," A SOLDIER SAID "THAT THE EMPEROR IS VISITING OUR PROVINCE. THIS IS A CASE FOR HIS AUGUST DECISION"

THE CAPTAIN ANSWERED: "THERE CAN BE ONLY ONE VERDICT——DEATH!"
NEXT WEEK: THE FORBIDDEN EMPIRE

70   Tarzan and the Chinese

Tarzan

by EDGAR RICE BURROUGHS

THE FORBIDDEN EMPIRE

INTO A STRANGE TOWN TARZAN WAS LED, THROUGH MYSTERIOUS STREETS TO THE PROVINCIAL PALACE OF THE EMPEROR.

THERE IN A VAST HALL THAT BORE WITNESS TO A SUPERB CULTURE, SAT SUN TAI, MONARCH AND SCHOLAR IN MAJESTIC SPLENDOR. THE EMPEROR LIFTED HIS EYES IN SURPRISE. NEVER HAD HE SEEN SUCH A CREATURE AS TARZAN.

THE APE-MAN'S CAPTORS FELL UPON THEIR KNEES IN OBEISANCE TO THE AUGUST ONE.

BUT TARZAN REMAINED ERECT. THE MIGHTY LORD OF THE JUNGLE KNELT TO NO MAN.

UP SPRANG THE CAPTAIN OF THE GUARD AND SIGNALLED TO TARZAN TO KNEEL.

THEN THE CAPTAIN RAISED HIS SWORD TO CLEAVE THE STRANGER WHO REFUSED HOMAGE TO THE ILLUSTRIOUS ONE.

BUT THE EMPEROR WITH AN INDULGENT SMILE WAVED THE OFFICER ASIDE AND BECKONED TARZAN TO HIM.

LIKE MANY CIVILIZED MEN, SUN TAI ADMIRED THIS STALWART CREATURE WHO WAS SO PLAINLY A BROTHER TO NATURE.

NOW THE GUARDS RELATE HOW TARZAN HAD CROSSED THE BARRIER OF BEASTS TO ENTER THE FORBIDDEN EMPIRE.

SUN TAI FROWNED. HE LIKED THIS BARBARIAN; YET, ACCORDING TO ANCIENT LAW, INTRUDERS MUST DIE!

MANY A TIME TARZAN HAD OUTWITTED SAVAGE CAPTORS, BUT COULD HIS JUNGLE ARTS COPE WITH THESE ENLIGHTENED MEN?

NEXT WEEK:
THE HEADSMAN

HOGARTH—

Tarzan

by EDGAR RICE BURROUGHS

THE HEADSMAN

SUN TAI WISHED TO SPARE TARZAN. BUT DEATH WAS THE PENALTY CITED IN THE SACRED BOOK OF ANCESTORS.

AGES AGO THE FORBIDDEN EMPIRE HAD ISOLATED ITSELF FROM BARBARIANS SUCH AS THIS ONE.

NOW THE EMPEROR SPOKE IN A SAD, SMALL VOICE: "SUMMON THE HEADSMAN. THE INTRUDER MUST DIE!"

PRESENTLY THERE WAS A FLUTTER IN THE HALL. A MASKED GIANT STALKED IN BEARING A MAMMOTH SWORD.

TARZAN HAD UNDERSTOOD NO WORD OF THE PROCEEDINGS, BUT THERE COULD BE NO MISTAKE. THIS WAS THE EXECUTIONER.

THE APE-MAN GLANCED ABOUT HIM. NOW WAS THE TIME TO ESCAPE, IF HE WERE TO ESCAPE AT ALL.

SUDDENLY HE LUNGED AT THE CIRCLE OF GUARDSMEN. TWO FELL TO THE FLOOR, BUT OTHERS POUNCED ON HIM.

THE JUNGLE LORD SHOOK FREE. THESE SOLDIERS, WEAKENED BY THE EASE OF CIVILIZATION WERE NO TRUE FIGHTING MEN.

SUN TAI LOOKED ON IN ADMIRATION. WHEN TARZAN BROKE AWAY HE COULD BARELY CONCEAL HIS DELIGHT.

BUT NOW A QUICK-MINDED COURTIER TOOK OFF HIS ROBE AND FLUNG IT OVER THE APE-MAN'S HEAD. THUS BLINDED, TARZAN WAS EASILY OVERWHELMED; AND AS THE SOLDIERS HELD HIM—

HOGARTH—

—THE HEADSMAN CLAPPED A HAND UPON HIS SHOULDER TO CLAIM HIM. NEXT WEEK: A FRIEND AND A FOE

383-7-10-38

Tarzan

A FRIEND
AND
A FOE

by EDGAR RICE BURROUGHS

© 1938 Edgar Rice Burroughs, Inc.—Trade Mark Reg. U. S. Pat.
Off. Produced by Famous Books and Plays. Distributed by
UNITED FEATURE SYNDICATE, Inc.

AS THE HEADSMAN LAID HOLD OF TARZAN, THERE WAS A SUDDEN STIR AT A DOORWAY.

THEN, THROUGH A LANE OF COURTIERS WALKED A GIRL OF STARTLING BEAUTY, ROBED IN REGAL GRANDEUR.

"COME, LULING, MY DAUGHTER," THE EMPEROR SMILED; "IT IS WELL THAT YOU BE ACQUAINTED WITH AFFAIRS OF STATE."

THE GIRL PAID NO HEED TO HER FATHER'S WORDS; HER EYES WERE FIXED IN FASCINATION ON THE HANDSOME APE-MAN.

TARZAN WAS A MAN OF STOIC CALM. BUT HE LOOKED WITH FASCINATION UPON THIS ENCHANTING CREATURE. LULING TURNED TO HER FATHER. "MUST HE DIE?" SHE SIGHED. "IT IS SO WRITTEN," SUN TAI EXPLAINED SADLY.

THE FIRST SPARKS OF LOVE WERE KINDLING THE GIRL'S HEART—AND HER MIND. SUDDENLY SHE CRIED OUT. "THE LAW OF OUR ANCESTORS DECREES JUSTICE. IS IT JUST TO CONDEMN A MAN WHO CANNOT SPEAK IN HIS OWN DEFENSE?"

"NO!" SUN TAI CHUCKLED; "SO THE STRANGER MUST BE REPRIEVED UNTIL HE CAN LEARN OUR LANGUAGE."

"OURS MUST BE A DIFFICULT TONGUE FOR A BARBARIAN," LULING SMILED DREAMILY; "HIS EDUCATION WILL BE SLOW."

THE MOST INTENT OBSERVER OF THIS DRAMA WAS PRINCE FANG CHU-FANG, GENERAL OF THE ARMIES AND LULING'S SUITOR.

HOGARTH—

NEXT WEEK. THE HORSEMEN OF DOOM!

JEALOUSY SEARED HIS EVIL HEART. HE VOWED ENMITY TO TARZAN AND FANG WAS A CRAFTY, VICIOUS FOE!

Tarzan
by EDGAR RICE BURROUGHS

THE HORSEMEN OF DOOM

"THE PRISONER IS REPRIEVED," THE EMPEROR DECREED; "UNTIL HE CAN LEARN OUR LANGUAGE AND DEFEND HIMSELF."

THE GLAMOUROUS PRINCESS SMILED. HER PLEA HAD SAVED THE FASCINATING STRANGER --- FOR A TIME, AT LEAST.

IN THE DAYS THAT FOLLOWED, THE FRIENDLY SOVEREIGN TOOK EAGER INTEREST IN THE "BARBARIAN."

HE INSTRUCTED TARZAN IN HIS LANGUAGE SO THAT HE MIGHT LEARN OF THE WORLD BEYOND HIS FORBIDDEN EMPIRE.

LU-LING BECAME A TEACHER, TOO; BUT HER INTEREST CENTERED IN THE ROMANTIC APE-MAN HIMSELF.

TARZAN LEARNED QUICKLY, BUT THE ROYAL TUTORS CUNNINGLY CONCEALED HIS PROGRESS FROM OUTSIDERS.

SOON THE JUNGLE LORD TIRED OF THIS LIFE OF IDYLLIC EASE. HIS ADVENTUROUS SPIRIT HUNGERED FOR ACTION.

HE HAD NOT LONG TO WAIT. ONE DAY A COURTIER DASHED BREATHLESSLY INTO THE ROYAL APARTMENTS.

"THE BANDITS!" HE CRIED; "THE DREADFUL BANDITS OF CHANG-LOON; THE HORSEMEN OF DOOM! THEY'RE UPON US!"

THEN TARZAN SAW THEM—A WILD THUNDERING TROOP, RIDING LIKE DEMONS.

"THE EMPEROR! THE EMPEROR!" THE BANDITS YELLED; "WE'VE COME TO TAKE THE EMPEROR!"

TARZAN LEAPED UP. THE URGE TO BATTLE FIRED HIS BLOOD. THE EMPEROR WAS HIS FRIEND, TO BE DEFENDED WITH HIS LIFE!

NEXT WEEK: THE BANDITS' RAID!

HOGARTH—

Tarzan
by EDGAR RICE BURROUGHS

THE BANDIT'S RAID

THE HORSEMEN OF DOOM THUNDERED FULL TILT TOWARD THE PALACE TO CAPTURE THE EMPEROR.

IN AMAZEMENT TARZAN SAW THE ROYAL GUARDSMEN SLAM THE GATES, AND FLEE.

HE TURNED QUICKLY TO THE EMPEROR. "YOUR SOLDIERS DO NOT FIGHT----THEY RUN AWAY!"

"THE BANDITS ARE STRONGER," SUN TAI SHRUGGED; "A WISE MAN BOWS TO THE INEVITABLE."

ALREADY THE OUTLAWS WERE RAMMING THE GATES. SOON THEY FELL, AND THE TURBULENT HORDE ENTERED.

FRIGHTENED COURTIERS RAN TO THE ROYAL APARTMENTS WHERE THE EMPEROR STOOD CALM, RESIGNED TO CAPTURE.

PRESENTLY THE CLAMOROUS FOOTSTEPS OF THE BANDITS RESOUNDED IN THE CORRIDOR.

"WILL YOU NOT DEFEND YOURSELVES?" TARZAN ASKED. SUN TAI SHOOK HIS HEAD.

"CIVILIZED MEN SCORN VIOLENCE. ONLY BAR-BARIANS AND RUDE BANDITS FIGHT. I'LL BE CAPTURED AND PAY THE RANSOM."

"THE WISE MAN FIGHTS THE BEAST THAT ATTACKS HIM," TARZAN DECLARED GRIMLY.

THEN HE SEIZED ONE OF THE SWORDS THAT HUNG AS DECORATIONS ON THE WALLS.

HOGARTH

NEXT WEEK: -CAPTURED-

AND AS THE RAIDERS BROKE DOWN THE DOOR, TARZAN STOOD ALONE AGAINST THE FOE!

Tarzan

by EDGAR RICE BURROUGHS

CAPTURED

TARZAN STOOD ALONE AGAINST THE SURGING FOE, HIS SWORD FLASHING POWERFUL, EFFECTIVE STROKES. BUT THE BANDITS DROVE HIM SLOWLY BACK.

TO SUN TAI, PEACE WAS THE HIGHEST VIRTUE; ALWAYS HE HAD HELD FIGHTING IN CONTEMPT.

BUT THE SIGHT OF TARZAN'S HEROIC STRUGGLE STRIPPED AWAY HIS ANCIENT HERITAGE OF CIVILIZATION.

IN HIS BLOOD STIRRED THE PRIMITIVE URGE TO FIGHT, TO DEFEND HIMSELF AND LULING. HE SEIZED A SWORD.

THE COURTIERS, TOO, INSPIRED BY THEIR SOVEREIGN, TOOK UP SWORDS, AND FOLLOWED HIM TO THE FRAY.

AND THEY FELL BACK UNDER THE ONSLAUGHT OF THE DARING OUTLAWS.

BUT LONG DEVOTION TO THE REFINEMENTS OF LIVING HAD WEAKENED THEIR VALUE AS FIGHTING MEN.

EVEN THE MIGHTY TARZAN, WHO FOUGHT AS A DOZEN MEN, COULD NOT STEM THE TIDE.

AT LAST THE EMPEROR, PRINCESS LULING, AND TARZAN WERE TAKEN PRISONER.

HOGARTH—

THEN THE OUTLAWS TOSSED THEM ACROSS THE BACKS OF THREE HORSES, AND GALLOPED AWAY TO THEIR LAIR IN THE DISTANT HILLS.

NEXT WEEK: TARZAN'S DOOM!

387-8-7-38

Tarzan

by EDGAR RICE BURROUGHS

TARZAN'S DOOM

INTO THE HILLS DASHED THE BANDITS WITH THEIR PRISONERS: TARZAN, THE EMPEROR, AND HIS DAUGHTER.

AND FROM THEIR ISOLATED LAIR, THE CHIEFTAIN DISPATCHED A NOTE DEMANDING RANSOM FOR SUN TAI AND LULING.

BUT FOR THE MIGHTY TARZAN HE HAD OTHER PLANS. "I WILL MAKE YOU MY LIEUTENANT," HE OFFERED.

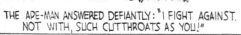

THE APE-MAN ANSWERED DEFIANTLY: "I FIGHT AGAINST, NOT WITH, SUCH CUTTHROATS AS YOU!"

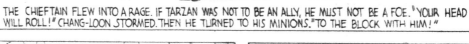

THE CHIEFTAIN FLEW INTO A RAGE. IF TARZAN WAS NOT TO BE AN ALLY, HE MUST NOT BE A FOE. "YOUR HEAD WILL ROLL!" CHANG-LOON STORMED. THEN HE TURNED TO HIS MINIONS. "TO THE BLOCK WITH HIM!"

THE OUTLAWS SEIZED TARZAN AND BORE HIM TO THE PLACE OF EXECUTION.

NO PLEA, NO WORD OF COMPLAINT PASSED HIS LIPS AS HE WAS BOUND TO STAKES, HIS NECK ON THE FATAL BLOCK.

IN TREMULOUS DISMAY, LULING WHISPERED TO HER FATHER.

THEN SUN TAI SPOKE: "SPARE THE STRANGER. THE IMPERIAL TREASURY WILL PAY WHAT RANSOM YOU DEMAND."

HOGARTH—

CHANG-LOON SHOOK HIS HEAD. TARZAN WAS TOO DANGEROUS TO BE ALLOWED TO LIVE.

NEXT WEEK:
THE DEMON BEASTS

SO HE STRODE GRIMLY TO THE EXECUTION BLOCK AND RAISED HIS MAMMOTH SWORD!

Tarzan

by EDGAR RICE BURROUGHS

THE DEMON BEASTS

AS THE BANDIT CHIEF PREPARED TO SEVER TARZAN'S HEAD HE WAS STARTLED BY THE FEARFUL ROARING OF LIONS.

TERRIFIED, CHANG-LOON DROPPED HIS SWORD AND FLED, FOLLOWED BY HIS BANDITS. IN THEIR PANIC THEY FORGOT THE CAPTIVES.

TO THE PEOPLE OF THIS STRANGE LAND, LIONS WERE INVINCIBLE DEMONS, WHICH NO MAN DARED DEFY.

BUT SUN TAI AND LULING, INSTEAD OF JOINING THE WILD STAMPEDE, RAN TO TARZAN.

AS THEY WORKED FRANTICALLY TO FREE HIM, A PACK OF HUNTING LIONS BURST FROM THE FOREST.

THE EMPEROR AND HIS DAUGHTER BELIEVED ALL THREE WERE DOOMED, BUT THEY DID NOT CEASE THEIR EFFORTS.

SUDDENLY, WITH A MIGHTY SURGE OF POWER, TARZAN BROKE THE REMAINING BONDS.

QUICKLY HE SEIZED SUN TAI AND LULING, AND CARRIED THEM TO A CLUSTER OF TREES.

AND WHILE THE LIONS BORE DOWN ON THEM, HE TRANSFERRED THEM TO SAFETY.

"THEY ARE STUBBORN CREATURES," SUN TAI SIGHED, "THEY MAY REMAIN UNTIL WE ARE FORCED TO DESCEND."

MOST OF THE BEASTS RUSHED PAST-BUT THREE REMAINED TO IMPRISON THE FUGITIVES IN THE TREES.

HOGARTH—

"I'LL DRIVE THEM AWAY," TARZAN SAID SIMPLY, AND DOWN HE DROPPED TO FACE THE DEMON BEASTS!

NEXT WEEK: NATURE'S BROTHER

Tarzan
by EDGAR RICE BURROUGHS

"NATURE'S BROTHER"

AS ONE OF THE LIONS CHARGED, TARZAN DODGED, WHEELED AND LEAPED ASTRIDE THE RAGING CARNIVORE.

THOUGH THE BEAST REARED TO SHAKE HIM OFF, TARZAN CLUNG TIGHTLY, DRIVING HIS KNIFE INTO THE TAWNY HIDE.

THE CREATURE FELL DEAD: BUT NOW THE TWO REMAINING LIONS CHARGED AT ONCE.

IN THE TREES ABOVE, LU LING SCREAMED, BELIEVING HER HERO WAS SURELY DOOMED.

NOW TARZAN LIFTED THE CARCASS OF THE FALLEN BEAST AND HURLED IT INTO THE FACE OF THE LEADING ASSAILANT.

THE OTHER RACED ON, BUT TARZAN MET HIM AND SLEW HIM AS HE HAD THE FIRST.

THEN THE THIRD, BRIEFLY HALTED, RESUMED HIS CHARGE. TARZAN STOOD STAUNCH, VOICING FEROCIOUS GROWLS. THE LION STOPPED, THEN TURNED AND TROTTED AWAY. THE MIGHTY APE-MAN HAD BLUFFED THE KING OF BEASTS.

ABOVE, SUN TAI, THE SCHOLAR MUSED: "AS A WEAPON AGAINST EVIL, THERE IS VIRTUE IN SUCH PHYSICAL PROWESS."

SO RETURNING TO THE IMPERIAL CITY, SUN TAI DECREED FOR TARZAN THE HOMAGE RESERVED FOR POETS AND SAGES. AND THE PEOPLE, WHO HAD ALWAYS STRESSED THE ARTS OF THE MIND UNITED TO HONOR "NATURE'S BROTHER."

BUT FANG CHU-FANG, TARZAN'S FOE, VOWED THAT HIS HONORS--AND HIS LIFE--WOULD SOON BE CUT SHORT! NEXT WEEK---- A BID TO DISASTER!

Tarzan

by EDGAR RICE BURROUGHS

A BID TO DISASTER

FANG'S ENMITY SOON BORE FRUIT. ON HIS DEMAND TARZAN WAS PUT ON TRIAL FOR ENTERING THE FORBIDDEN EMPIRE.

HOPING TO SAVE TARZAN, THE EMPEROR PROMPTED HIM. "YOU CAME HERE BY ERROR, DIDN'T YOU?"

"NO," REPLIED THE APE-MAN; "I CAME TO SEE WHAT WAS HERE." EVEN TO SAVE HIS LIFE HE WOULD NOT LIE.

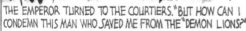

THE EMPEROR TURNED TO THE COURTIERS. "BUT HOW CAN I CONDEMN THIS MAN WHO SAVED ME FROM THE "DEMON LIONS?"

"STRANGERS MUST DIE!" FANG INSISTED. "SUCH IS THE IMMUTABLE LAW OF OUR ANCESTORS."

SADLY, SUN TAI SUMMONED THE HEADSMAN. PRINCESS LULING WEPT, FOR SHE LOVED THE STALWART "BARBARIAN."

BUT SUDDENLY HER TEARFUL EYES LIT UP. SHE WHISPERED TO HER FATHER, WHO CRIED OUT JOYOUSLY:-- "I HEREBY ADOPT TARZAN; NOW HE IS MY SON, NO LONGER A STRANGER. HE NEED NOT DIE!"

COURTIERS HAILED THE WISE DECISION AND SUN TAI DECREED A JUBILEE THROUGHOUT THE LAND.

BUT THESE HAPPY FESTIVALS WERE AN INVITATION TO DISASTER BECAUSE----

--THEIR SPLENDOR WAS VIEWED FROM A HILLTOP ACROSS THE BORDER BY HIYEDO, CHIEF OF THE WARLIKE AIYUS.

AND HIS SAVAGE HEART HUNGERED TO CONQUER THAT RICH AND PEACEFUL LAND.

NEXT WEEK: DEVIL POWDER

80   Tarzan and the Chinese

Tarzan

by EDGAR RICE BURROUGHS

DEVIL POWDER

HIYEDO, BARBARIAN WAR LORD, GAZED WITH GREEDY EYES UPON THE RICH FORBIDDEN EMPIRE, WHILE ---

---- FAR AWAY, LOI WAN, COURT WIZARD, PLANNED A SENSATIONAL SPECTACLE IN TARZAN'S HONOR.

BEFORE A VAST ASSEMBLY, LOI WAN ASCENDED A HILL, BURIED A TINY PACKET, LIGHTED A FUSE, AND RAN.

A MINUTE LATER, THE HILLTOP EXPLODED WITH VOLCANIC FORCE AND MAGNIFICENCE.

WHILE THE PEOPLE CHEERED WITH DELIGHT, THE ASTONISHED APE-MAN ASKED THE WIZARD: "WHAT IS IT?"

"A PINCH OF MY NEW DEVIL POWDER," LOI WAN SMILED; "I SHALL USE IT TO DISPEL EVIL SPIRITS."

BUT TARZAN KNEW HE HAD WITNESSED THE BIRTH OF THE MOST POWERFUL EXPLOSIVE KNOWN.

HOW FORTUNATE THAT ITS SECRET WAS LOCKED IN THIS PEACE-FUL LAND, WHERE IT WOULD NEVER BE USED FOR HUMAN DESTRUCTION.

MEANWHILE, HIYEDO, PEERING THROUGH STOLEN BINOCULARS, REALIZED THE MEANING OF THE TERRIFIC EXPLOSIVE.

"IF I COULD GET THAT," HE GROWLED, "I'D CONQUER THE WORLD!" ONE OF HIS AIDES SHOOK HIS HEAD. "TWICE WE'VE ATTACKED THE FORBIDDEN EMPIRE; AND TWICE WE'VE BEEN STOPPED BY THE BARRIER OF BEASTS."

"THIS TIME I HAVE A PLAN THAT CANNOT FAIL," THE WAR LORD THUNDERED. "DESTINY BECKONS HIYEDO!"

NEXT WEEK: INVASION

—HOGARTH—

Tarzan

INVASION

by EDGAR RICE BURROUGHS

HIYEDO RAISED A MIGHTY FORCE TO ASSAULT THE FORBIDDEN EMPIRE WHICH WAS GUARDED BY THE BARRIER OF BEASTS.

THEY MARCHED TO THE FIRST WALL AND SCALED IT BY A HUNDRED LADDERS. THEN PART OF THE ARMY----

---FORMED STRONG RANKS, WITH A LANE BETWEEN, ACROSS THE LION-INFESTED NO-MAN'S LAND.

THE BEASTS ATTACKED, MANY WARRIORS DIED, BUT MOST OF THEM PASSED SAFELY DOWN THE LANE.

ONCE PAST THE BARRIER, HIYEDO BEGAN HIS MERCILESS MARCH, KILLING AND LOOTING.

TO THE EMPEROR CAME A FLEET MESSENGER, CRYING NEWS OF THE BARBARIAN INVASION.

SUN TAI COMMANDED GENERAL FANG TO MOBILIZE HIS MEAGER ARMY. FANG HESITATED, KNOWING DEFEAT WAS CERTAIN.

"LET US SURRENDER, AND SAVE OUR LAND AND LIVES," HE URGED. SUN TAI REFLECTED, AND NODDED PAINFUL ASSENT.

THEN TARZAN SPOKE UP GRIMLY. "DEATH IS BETTER THAN SLAVERY. WE MUST FIGHT."

SUN TAI'S EYES LIGHTED. ONCE MORE HE FELL UNDER THE SPELL OF TARZAN'S GALLANT SPIRIT.

"SO BE IT," HE CRIED; "YOU, TARZAN, SHALL LEAD THE ARMY, WITH FANG AS YOUR AIDE!" FANG'S PRIDE WAS STABBED, BUT HE FORESAW A CHANCE FOR REVENGE AGAINST THE MAN HE HATED!

NEXT WEEK:
THE TRAITOR

HOGARTH—

Tarzan

by Edgar Rice Burroughs

Copr. 1938 Edgar Rice Burroughs Inc.—The Reg. U.S. Pat.
Off. Produced by Famous Funny and Plays, Distributed by
UNITED FEATURE SYNDICATE, Inc.

THE TRAITOR

AT THE EMPEROR'S COMMAND, TARZAN MOBILIZED THE MEAGER ARMY TO RESIST THE INVADING HORDE.

WITH HEAVY HEART HE INSPECTED THE ILL-TRAINED TROOPS, NEGLECTED THROUGH YEARS OF PEACE

THEN HE RODE AWAY, WHILE PRINCESS LULING WEPT, BELIEVING HER HERO WOULD NEVER RETURN.

ON THE PLAINS OF NAKON BUREE, TARZAN'S SCANTY ARMY ENCOUNTERED THE INVADING BARBARIANS.

HIYEDO LAUGHED HE WAS SURE HIS SAVAGE FORCE WOULD SOON WIPE OUT THIS UNWARLIKE SOLDIERY.

BUT AT THE FIRST CLASH, TARZAN'S MEN, INSPIRED BY HIS OWN EXAMPLE, BECAME FIGHTING FIENDS.

AND THEY WERE FIRED BY THE IDEAL OF DEFENDING THEIR ANCIENT CULTURE AGAINST THE BRUTAL BARBARIANS

BUT FANG CHU-FANG, TARZAN'S AIDE AND SECRET ENEMY THOUGHT ONLY OF SAVING HIS OWN LIFE.

TARZAN'S MEN FOUGHT DOGGEDLY, BUT THEY WERE FORCED SLOWLY BACK BY OVERWHELMING NUMBERS

NIGHT FELL ON THE BLOODY BATTLEFIELD AND THE TWO ARMIES CAMPED TO AWAIT THE DAWN.

NOW CAME FANG'S CHANCE TO TAKE HIS LONG-AWAITED REVENGE ON TARZAN AND WIN A REWARD FOR HIMSELF!

HOGARTH→

QUIETLY HE SLIPPED AWAY— TO MAKE A TREACHEROUS BARGAIN WITH THE FOE!

NEXT WEEK: **TARZAN CAPTURED**

Tarzan and the Chinese   83

Tarzan

by EDGAR RICE BURROUGHS

394-9-25-38

Cop. 1938 Edgar Rice Burroughs Inc.—Trd. Reg. U.S. Pat.
Off. Produced by Fathers, Reels and Plays. Distributed by
UNITED FEATURE SYNDICATE, Inc.

TARZAN CAPTURED

FANG CHU-FANG SLIPPED STEALTHILY ACROSS TO THE ENEMY LINES.

A SENTRY SEIZED HIM AND TOOK HIM TO HIYEDO, WHICH WAS DESIRED, FOR NOW----

---HE BROACHED HIS TREACHEROUS PLAN TO THE INVADING CHIEFTAIN.

"TOMORROW I'LL TURN THE BATTLE IN YOUR FAVOR, IF YOU WILL SET ME UP ON SUN TAI'S THRONE."

HIYEDO AGREED EAGERLY. HE WOULD BE A GREAT EMPEROR; FANG WOULD BE THE PUPPET KING OF THE PROVINCE.

AT DAWN THE BLOODY CONFLICT WAS RESUMED BETWEEN HIYEDO'S SAVAGES AND TARZAN'S BRAVE DEFENDERS.

ONCE MORE THE MIGHTY JUNGLE LORD INSPIRED HIS MEN TO HEROIC ACTION.

THEIR FIRST FURIOUS IMPACT HURLED BACK THE INVADERS. THEN FANG FULFILLED HIS TREACHEROUS PACT.

HE ORDERED HIS OWN BATTALION TO RETIRE, THUS LEAVING TARZAN'S SECTOR EXPOSED.

SWEEPING IN QUICKLY, HIYEDO'S SAVAGES SURROUNDED THE APE-MAN AND A CLUSTER OF HIS FOLLOWERS.

TARZAN FOUGHT VALIANTLY TO CUT HIS WAY OUT.

HOGARTH—

BUT AT LAST HE FELL INTO THE HANDS OF THE ENEMY
NEXT WEEK: **DOOMED TO DIE!**

Tarzan

by Edgar Rice Burroughs

DOOMED TO DIE!

BETRAYED BY FANG CHU-FANG, TARZAN FELL SWIFTLY INTO THE HANDS OF THE ENEMY.

HIS MEN CHARGED IN TO HELP HIM, BUT THE SAVAGES BEAT THEM BACK.

WITHOUT HIS SKILFUL LEADERSHIP, TARZAN REALIZED, HIS TROOPS WOULD BE SLAUGHTERED.

"RUN!" HE SHOUTED; "YOU CANNOT SAVE ME. SAVE YOUR-SELVES!" AND SO HIS ARMY FLED.

THEN, WITH TARZAN A PRISONER, HIYEDO, THE BARBARIAN CONQUEROR, MARCHED ON UNOPPOSED.

WHEN THE APE-MAN'S SHATTERED FORCES REACHED THE CAPITAL, THE CITY WAS SEIZED WITH PANIC.

SUN TAI FLED TO THE HINTERLAND WITH HIS COURT AND THE REMNANT OF HIS ARMY.

BUT THE PEOPLE, ATTACHED TO THEIR HOMES, REMAINED, WHILE-------

--THE RUTHLESS HIYEDO MADE HIS TRIUMPHAL ENTRY.

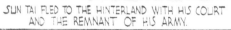

THE BARBARIAN CHIEF DESIRED TO SHOW WHAT HAPPENED TO THOSE WHO OPPOSED HIM.

NEXT WEEK: A HUMAN TARGET

SO HE COMMANDED THAT TARZAN BE TAKEN TO THE GREAT PLAZA, WHERE A SQUAD OF SAVAGES RANGED THEMSELVES BEFORE HIM, TO HURL THEIR SPEARS UNTIL THE APE-MAN DROPPED.

HOGARTH-

Tarzan

by Edgar Rice Burroughs

A HUMAN TARGET

CALMLY TARZAN FACED THE SQUAD OF SPEARMEN WHO HAD BEEN ASSIGNED TO KILL HIM, WHILE----

---THE POPULACE OF THE CONQUERED CITY, ASSEMBLED BY HIYEDO'S COMMAND, LOOKED ON IN DESPAIR.

THE APE-MAN WAS UNFETTERED, BECAUSE FREEDOM TO DODGE MADE HIM A MORE EXCITING TARGET.

CONFIDENTLY, THE FIRST SPEARMAN CAST HIS LANCE.

TARZAN DARTED ASIDE; HIS HAND FLASHED OUT LIKE LIGHTNING, AND GRASPED THE SPEEDING MISSILE.

INSTANTLY HE HURLED IT BACK INTO THE RANKS OF HIS EXECUTIONERS.

ONE OF THE SAVAGES FELL, THE SPEAR THROUGH HIS SIDE!

A STARTLED CRY WENT UP, AND IN THE CONFUSION, TARZAN FLED ACROSS THE PLAZA.

THE CROWDS TRIED TO OPEN A WAY FOR HIM, FOR HE WAS THEIR HERO.

BUT SO GREAT WAS THE PRESS OF PEOPLE THAT HIS FLIGHT WAS IMPEDED.

HOGARTH—

HIYEDO CALLED TO HIS SOLDIERS; "HE'S TRAPPED! BRING HIM BACK!"

THEN THE HOWLING SAVAGES WEDGED INTO THE THRONG AND BROUGHT THE FUGITIVE TO BAY.
NEXT WEEK: **BOUND FOR DISASTER**

Tarzan

by EDGAR RICE BURROUGHS

BOUND FOR DISASTER

TARZAN'S CAPTURE SEEMED CERTAIN WHEN THE SOLDIERS HEMMED HIM AGAINST THE SIDE OF A BUILDING.

BUT THE APE-MAN CLAMBERED UP THE WALL, AND WAS SOON BEYOND THE REACH OF THE UP-FLUNG SPEARS.

PRESENTLY HE VANISHED OVER THE ROOF.

HIYEDO AND FANG WERE UNDISTURBED FOR THEY BELIEVED TARZAN POWERLESS TO BLOCK THEIR SCHEMES.

IMMEDIATELY THE TRAITOR FANG WAS SET UP AS PUPPET KING UNDER HIYEDO'S EMPERORSHIP.

HIYEDO'S GOAL NOW WAS TO ACQUIRE THE MIRACULOUS EXPLOSIVE THAT HAD LURED HIM HERE.

SO FANG WENT TO LOI WAN THE WIZARD, AND FORCED HIM TO REVEAL THE FORMULA FOR THE DEVIL POWDER

THEN HE TREACHEROUSLY KILLED LOI WAN, AND BECAME SOLE POSSESSOR OF THE DREADFUL SECRET.

NOW FANG SET UP A GREAT ARSENAL WHERE THE INFERNAL POWDER WAS PREPARED.

HIYEDO URGED HASTE WITH THIS NEW WEAPON HE DREAMED OF CONQUERING THE WORLD.

MEANWHILE-- TARZAN RALLIED HIS FUGITIVE FORCES TO REDEEM THE CONQUERED CITY-----

----NEVER REALIZING THAT HE WAS LEADING THEM TO A THUNDEROUS, SHATTERING DOOM! NEXT WEEK: FANG'S POWER

HOGARTH—

Tarzan

by Edgar Rice Burroughs

Copr. 1938 Edgar Rice Burroughs, Inc.—Reg. U.S. Pat.
Off. Produced by Famous Books and Plays. Distributed by
UNITED FEATURE SYNDICATE, Inc

THE DEVIL-POWDER ARSENAL

THE BLASTS WHICH FELLED TARZAN NOW STIRRED HIM FROM HIS COMA.

HE SAW HIS MEN DASHING RECKLESSLY INTO THE INFERNO OF EXPLOSIVES.

BY SHOUTS AND SIGNS HE COMMANDED THEM TO RETREAT TO AVOID ANNIHILATION.

AND NOW, WITH THE REMNANT OF HIS FORCES, TARZAN FLED.

ONLY ONE HOPE REMAINED. TARZAN KNEW HE MUST DESTROY THE DEVIL POWDER FACTORY.

THAT NIGHT HE SLIPPED INTO THE CITY AND SEARCHED OUT THE TALL STRUCTURE WHERE THE EXPLOSIVES WERE MADE.

ELUDING THE GUARDS, HE SCALED THE OUTER WALL.

PRESENTLY HE LEAPED INTO THE APARTMENT OF FANG CHU-FANG HIS DEADLY FOE.

FANG SCREAMED. TARZAN DASHED FORWARD TO THROTTLE HIM.

TARZAN FOUGHT VALIANTLY, BUT AT LAST HE WAS OVERWHELMED.

BUT A CORPS OF GUARDS, FIERCE AND POWERFUL, BURST INTO THE ROOM.

HOGARTH—

NEXT WEEK: TRAPPED!

FANG CHUCKLED. "ONLY ONE PROBLEM REMAINS—— TO DECIDE THE MANNER OF YOUR DEATH!"

400-11-6-38.

Tarzan
by EDGAR RICE BURROUGHS

TRAPPED!

DELIGHTED WITH TARZAN'S CAPTURE, FANG BEGAN TO DEVISE FOR HIM A TORTUROUS DEATH!

THEN A SUDDEN INSPIRATION STRUCK HIM. HE WROTE A HURRIED NOTE AND DISPATCHED IT BY COURIER.

---TO PRINCESS LULING WHO READ; "TARZAN IS MY PRISONER. I SHALL SPARE HIM IF YOU WILL BE MY WIFE."

LULING HATED FANG, BUT SHE DID HIS BIDDING TO SAVE THE LIFE OF TARZAN, WHOM SHE LOVED.

WHEN SHE CAME TO HIS APARTMENT, FANG ORDERED TARZAN BROUGHT IN TO WITNESS HIS VILLAINOUS TRIUMPH.

"I HAVE COME TO BE YOUR WIFE," LULING SAID TEARFULLY; "NOW LET TARZAN GO FREE."

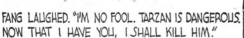

FANG LAUGHED. "I'M NO FOOL. TARZAN IS DANGEROUS. NOW THAT I HAVE YOU, I SHALL KILL HIM."

THEN HE EMBRACED THE GIRL. SHE STRUGGLED. BUT FANG CHUCKLED AT HER RESISTANCE.

TARZAN FLAMED WITH ANGER AT FANG'S TREACHERY, AND AT HIS MISTREATMENT OF LULING.

WITH A MIGHTY SURGE OF POWER HE BURST HIS BONDS. IF HE WAS TO DIE, HE'D DIE FIGHTING!

HOGARTH

HE LEAPED AT THE VILLAIN. FANG CRIED OUT. GUARDS BURST INTO THE ROOM. "KILL HIM!" SCREAMED FANG. AND THE GUARDS RUSHED TO OBEY! *NEXT WEEK: THE LAST STAND*

401-11-13-38

Tarzan
by Edgar Rice Burroughs

Copr. 1938 Edgar Rice Burroughs, Inc.—Tm. Reg. U. S. Pat.
Off. Produced by Famous Books and Plays. Distributed by
UNITED FEATURE SYNDICATE, Inc.

THE LAST STAND

AS THE GUARDS CHARGED, TARZAN DODGED, THEN DARTED IN AND WRESTED A SWORD FROM AN ADVERSARY.

SUDDENLY HIYEDO BURST INTO THE ROOM; AND TARZAN HEARD THE CLATTERING OF MORE SOLDIERS IN THE HALL.

HE LEAPED TO THE DOOR, LOCKED IT, FLUNG THE KEY OUT THE WINDOW. HE WOULD CONQUER OR DIE!

BACK TO THE WALL, TARZAN FOUGHT DESPERATELY, DEALING DOOM TO HIS ANTAGONISTS.

AT LAST ONLY HIYEDO REMAINED. THEN HE, TOO, FELL-----

---BUT AS HE TOPPLED, HIS SWORD KNOCKED A LAMP FROM THE WALL

OIL SPLASHED OUT, AND FLAMES RACED ALONG ITS SERPENTINE TRAIL. DRAPERIES CAUGHT FIRE. THE BLAZE SPREAD.

TARZAN KNEW THE FIRE WOULD SOON REACH THE STORES OF DEVIL POWDER. THE ARSENAL WOULD EXPLODE.

SEIZING LULING, HE RUSHED TO THE WINDOW AND CLIMBED HASTILY DOWN THE SIDE OF THE BUILDING.

FANG, WHO HAD BEEN COWERING IN A CORNER, SOUGHT TO FLEE THE INFERNO, BUT HIS ESCAPE WAS CUT OFF.

NOW THAT DEATH WAS INEVITABLE, HIS TERROR CHANGED TO FURY. "TARZAN WILL DIE, TOO!" HE SCREAMED.

SO, FROM A CHEST HE EXTRACTED A CYLINDER OF DEVIL POWDER, AND RAN TO THE WINDOW TO-----

HOGARTH-

---HURL THE DEADLY MISSILE AT TARZAN AND LULING FLEEING ACROSS THE PLAZA.

NEXT WEEK: **TOWARD NEW PERILS**

Tarzan

by EDGAR RICE BURROUGHS

Copr. 1939. Edgar Rice Burroughs, Inc.—Tm. Reg. U.S. Pat.
Off. Produced by Famous Books and Plays. Distributed by
UNITED FEATURE SYNDICATE, Inc.

TOWARD
NEW
PERILS

AS FANG RAISED HIS HAND TO HURL THE DEADLY DEVIL POWDER AT TARZAN AND LULING, THE ARSENAL EXPLODED WITH A TERRIFIC BLAST, THE MIGHTIEST THE WORLD HAD EVER SEEN.

BITS OF DEBRIS SHOWERED THE FUGITIVES, BUT TARZAN'S SWIFT FLIGHT HAD REMOVED THEM FROM THE DANGER ZONE.

"NOW THE SECRET OF THE DEVIL POWDER IS DESTROYED," THE APE-MAN SAID, "AND THE WORLD IS SPARED ITS TERRORS!"

LEADERLESS NOW, THE INVADERS FLED. AND MANY DIED AT THE BARRIER OF BEASTS THAT ENCIRCLED THE LAND OF SUN TAI.

THE REFUGEE EMPEROR RETURNED AMID GREAT REJOICING AND OFFERED TO MAKE TARZAN SUPREME WAR LORD.

BUT THE APE-MAN SHOOK HIS HEAD. HE HAD PERFORMED HIS MISSION. HE MUST BE ON HIS WAY ONCE MORE

LULING WEPT. SHE LOVED TARZAN BUT SHE COULD NOT HOLD HIS FREE, RESTLESS SPIRIT.

THAT NIGHT THE SOUNDS OF THE JUNGLE STIRRED THE APE-MAN'S BLOOD.

HE SLIPPED QUIETLY FROM THE CITY, ACROSS THE GREAT PLAIN TO THE BARRIER OF BEASTS.

THERE HE LEAPED TO THE TREES AND SPED OVER THE BARRIER WHILE SAVAGE LIONS ROARED BENEATH.

THEN ON INTO HIS BELOVED FOREST, LITTLE DREAMING OF THE AMAZING ADVENTURES HE WAS SOON TO ENCOUNTER NEXT WEEK: JUNGLE COMBAT

HOGARTH—

Tarzan

by Edgar Rice Burroughs

UNITED FEATURE SYNDICATE, Inc.

JUNGLE COMBAT

403-11-27-38

AFTER HIS LONG SOJOURN WITH CIVILIZED MEN, TARZAN EXULTED IN THE ELEMENTAL FOREST.

WHEN HE WAS HUNGRY, HE MADE A KILL AND ATE. WHEN HE WAS SLEEPY, HE CLIMBED TO A LOFTY TREE CROTCH AND SLEPT.

HE LOLLED ON THE BACK OF TANTOR, THE ELEPHANT. HE DEFIED MARAUDING LIONS. AGAIN HE WAS TARZAN, LORD OF THE JUNGLE.

ONE DAY HE CAME UPON A BAND OF APES. HE FELT THE URGE TO JOIN THEM, TO RELIVE THE DAYS OF HIS BOYHOOD.

WITHOUT WARNING, HE DROPPED DOWN AMONG THEM. THE GREAT APES GROWLED.

"I AM TARZAN," THE INTRUDER ANNOUNCED. BUT THESE BEASTS DID NOT KNOW HIM.

THEY WERE SURPRISED THAT A MAN-THING COULD SPEAK THEIR TONGUE. STILL, ALL MEN WERE ENEMIES.

NOW ONE HUGE BRUTE LUMBERED FORWARD. "I OGLUT, KING. OGLUT KILL!"

AS MONARCH OF THE WILDERNESS, TARZAN DARED NOT IGNORE THIS CHALLENGE TO HIS AUTHORITY.

"TARZAN MIGHTY FIGHTER. TARZAN KILL!" HE GROWLED, AND ADVANCED TOWARD HIS ADVERSARY.

THEN BEAST AND BEAST-MAN CLOSED IN FURIOUS COMBAT, WHICH COULD END ONLY IN SURRENDER OR DEATH.

TARZAN KNEW AT ONCE THE OUTCOME WAS IN DOUBT. HE HAD NEVER ENCOUNTERED AN APE SO POWERFUL. *NEXT WEEK: THE HAND OF FATE*

THE HAND OF
FATE

Tarzan
by EDGAR RICE BURROUGHS

OGLUT LOCKED HIS POWERFUL ARMS TO THROTTLE THE APE-MAN. BUT TARZAN BROKE AWAY, SEIZED THE APE-KING, FLUNG HIM OVER A SHOULDER, AND POUNCED FURIOUSLY ON HIM.

TARZAN'S ARMS CLAMPED THE CREATURE'S THROAT LIKE STEEL BANDS UNTIL OGLUT GASPED, "KAGODA—SURRENDER!"

THUS, ACCORDING TO CUSTOM, TARZAN BECAME KING OF THE TRIBE. AND WHILE HIS AWE-STRUCK SUBJECTS WATCHED—

---HE SPRANG TREEWARD TO EXHIBIT HIS STRENGTH AND AGILITY BY A SERIES OF SPECTACULAR LEAPS.

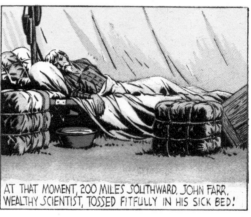

AT THAT MOMENT, 200 MILES SOUTHWARD, JOHN FARR, WEALTHY SCIENTIST, TOSSED FITFULLY IN HIS SICK BED!

HE HAD COME TO AFRICA TO SEEK THE "MISSING LINK" AND NOW HE WAS BALKED.

IN VAIN DID LINDA, HIS DAUGHTER, TRY TO ALLAY HIS IMPATIENCE.

FINALLY, SHE OFFERED TO PURSUE THE SEARCH WITH GREGOR MARSADA, THEIR GUIDE. HER FATHER AGREED.

HE CALLED MARSADA AND SAID: "FOR A SPECIMEN OF THE 'MISSING LINK' ALIVE, YOU'LL GET $100,000 — DEAD, $50,000!"

"AND HOW SHALL I RECOGNIZE THIS MISSING LINK?" MARSADA ASKED. JOHN FARR ANSWERED —

"HE'LL PROBABLY LOOK LIKE A MAN, BUT HE'LL SWING THROUGH THE TREES LIKE AN APE!"

HOGARTH—

NEXT WEEK:
—TARZAN'S ENEMY—

94   Tarzan and the Pygmies

405-12-11-38

Tarzan

by EDGAR RICE BURROUGHS

Copr. 1938 Edgar Rice Burroughs, Inc.—Trade Reg U.S. Pat
Off. Produced by Famous Books and Plays. Distributed by
UNITED FEATURE SYNDICATE, Inc

TARZAN'S ENEMY

LINDA AND MARSADA PUSHED ON THROUGH THE WILDERNESS IN SEARCH OF THE "MISSING LINK."
MARSADA GLANCED FREQUENTLY INTO THE TREES, FOR THERE, HE WAS TOLD, HE WOULD FIND HIS QUARRY.
AND TO THE KEEN EARS OF THE SENTINEL APE CAME THE SOUND OF THE SAFARI. HE HID IN THE BUSHES.

AND WHEN HE SAW THE MAN-THINGS MARCHING, HE RACED TO GIVE THE ALARM TO HIS FELLOWS WHO-----

--WERE FEEDING PEACEABLY WHILE TARZAN, THEIR NEW KING, TOOK A MIDDAY NAP IN THE TREES.

OGLUT, THE FORMER KING, WHOM TARZAN HAD CONQUERED, GAZED OFTEN ALOFT THROUGH HATE-FILLED EYES.

THE APE-MAN WAS SUDDENLY AROUSED BY A COMMOTION BELOW. HE DROPPED SWIFTLY TO EARTH.

THERE HE FOUND THE SENTINEL CRYING THE ALARM. "TARMANGANI! TARMANGANI! GOMANGANI! THUNDERSTICKS!"

"WE KILL!" GROWLED THE APES, WHO LOATHED THE MAN-THINGS AND THEIR GUNS.

TARZAN BADE THEM BE QUIET WHILE HE SCOUTED THE SAFARI TO DETERMINE THE DANGER.

HOGARTH—

"OGLUT GO WITH TARZAN," THE EX-KING GRUNTED. HE HOPED VAGUELY THAT ALONE IN THE FOREST----

NEXT WEEK:
A NEW DANGER

----HE MIGHT SOMEHOW HARM HIS RIVAL. HIS CHANCE WAS SOON TO COME!

Tarzan

by Edgar Rice Burroughs

Copr. 1938 Edgar Rice Burroughs Inc.—Reg. U. S. Pat.
Off. Produced by Famous Books and Plays. Distributed by
UNITED FEATURE SYNDICATE, Inc.

A NEW DANGER

TARZAN MOVED SWIFTLY THROUGH THE TREES TO INSPECT THE MYSTERIOUS SAFARI. WITH HIM WENT OGLUT, THE APE, HIS SECRET ENEMY, AWAITING A CHANCE TO HARM HIM.

SOON TARZAN CAUGHT THE SCENT OF MEN. THUS HE WAS GUIDED TO THE EDGE OF THE SAFARI CAMP.

THERE HE SAW TWO MEN, A WHITE AND A BLACK, RETURNING FROM A HUNT. HE DROPPED LOWER.

"THIS TARZAN'S COUNTRY," THE BLACK SAID FEARFULLY. MARSADA'S EYES BLAZED WITH EVIL DELIGHT.

ONCE TARZAN HAD AROUSED TRIBESMEN AGAINST HIM WHEN HE WAS STEALING IVORY. BUT TARZAN HAD REMAINED HIDDEN.

"HOW I'D LIKE TO LAY HANDS ON HIM," MARSADA SNARLED, "WOULD YOU RECOGNIZE HIM, BUTANO?"

"NO," THE BLACK REPLIED, "HE LIKE DEMON. MANY KNOW HIS DEEDS. FEW SEE HIM."

NOW MARSADA HAD A DOUBLE PURPOSE---TO DESTROY TARZAN, AND CAPTURE A SPECIMEN OF THE "MISSING LINK".

AS THE TWO STROLLED TOWARD CAMP, TARZAN AND OGLUT FOLLOWED QUIETLY THROUGH THE TREES.

FROM A TENT EMERGED LINDA FARR. "ANY TRACE OF THE 'MISSING LINK', MR. MARSADA?"

THE GUIDE SHOOK HIS HEAD. THEN SUDDENLY HE GLANCED INTO THE TREES WHERE TARZAN STOOD.

NEXT WEEK: A RASH VENTURE

HOGARTH—

Tarzan
by Edgar Rice Burroughs

A RASH VENTURE

AS MARSADA GLANCED UPWARD, TARZAN DODGED BACK, TOO QUICKLY TO BE DETECTED.

OGLUT GLOWERED, AS SOMETHING STIRRED IN HIS SLOW, DULL BRAIN. TO THE GREAT APES, RECKLESS, BOASTFUL BRAVERY WAS THE GREATEST VIRTUE.

OGLUT SLIPPED DOWN TO TARZAN'S SIDE. "TARZAN AFRAID," HE MUTTERED; "TARZAN NO GOOD KING."

TARZAN REALIZED HIS DILEMMA. OGLUT WOULD REPORT TO THE OTHER APES, WHO WOULD HOLD HIM IN CONTEMPT.

HE MUST MAKE SOME BOLD GESTURE, FOR HE MIGHT LOSE THE AUTHORITY BY WHICH HE RULED THE JUNGLE.

THE APE-MAN DREW HIMSELF UP PROUDLY. "TARZAN NOT AFRAID," HE SAID; "LOOK!"

AS HE SPOKE, HE SWOOPED DOWN THROUGH THE TREES, A WILD APE-CRY BURSTING FROM HIS LIPS.

THE EYES OF THE SAFARI PEOPLE SHOT UPWARD AND SAW THE STRANGE CREATURE FLITTING THROUGH THE TREES

THE BLACKS SCREAMED IN TERROR AT SIGHT OF THE MAN WHO TRAVELED LIKE AN APE.

LINDA FARR JOINED THEM IN THEIR VOCAL EXPRESSION OF ASTONISHMENT.

HOGARTH—

"THE 'MISSING LINK!'" CRIED MARSADA; "WE MUST GET HIM!"
NEXT WEEK:
TARZAN'S
— ENEMY —

408-1-1-39

Tarzan

by Edgar Rice Burroughs

Copr. 1938. Edgar Rice Burroughs Inc. Tm. Reg. U.S. Pat. Off. Produced at Tarzana Ranch and Films. Distributed by UNITED FEATURE SYNDICATE, Inc.

TARZAN'S ENEMY

TO PROVE HIS FEARLESSNESS TO OGLUT, TARZAN SWUNG DOWN BEFORE THE STARTLED EYES OF THE STRANGERS.

ALREADY HE WAS COUNTING THE RICH REWARD FOR CAPTURING A SPECIMEN OF THE "MISSING LINK."

"THERE!" SHOUTED MARSADA: "THE TREE-MAN! WE MUST TAKE HIM ALIVE!"

BUT TARZAN, AFTER HIS DARING FLOURISH, RETURNED TO CONCEALMENT.

"I'LL COAX HIM DOWN," MARSADA BOASTED. HE HURRIED TO HIS TENT AND REAPPEARED WITH—

—MIRRORS AND TRINKETS CALCULATED TO LURE THE PRIMITIVE CREATURE INTO HIS TRAP.

LOOKING DOWN ON THIS TRICKERY, TARZAN CONCEIVED A COLD DISLIKE FOR MARSADA.

HE RESOLVED TO CONFOUND, HARASS, AND ANNOY THIS EVIL INVADER OF HIS JUNGLE DOMAIN.

SO HE DROPPED DOWN TO A LOW BRANCH, TEASINGLY NEAR TO MARSADA.

BUT INSTEAD OF SHOWING INTEREST IN THE TRINKETS HIS EYES CAME TO REST ON THE BEAUTIFUL LINDA FARR.

A STRANGE FEELING CAME OVER THE GIRL. SHE WAS FRIGHTENED, YET OBVIOUSLY ENCHANTED BY THE APE-MAN.

HOGARTH—

A FIT OF JEALOUS RAGE SEIZED MARSADA. IMPULSIVELY HIS FINGERS TIGHTENED ON HIS RIFLE!
NEXT WEEK: **TARZAN'S MISFORTUNE**

Tarzan

by EDGAR RICE BURROUGHS

TARZAN'S MISFORTUNE

MARSADA WAS ENRAGED BY LINDA'S FASCINATED RESPONSE TO TARZAN'S GAZE. OFTEN HE HAD SOUGHT HER FAVOR, WITHOUT SUCCESS, AND NOW SHE SEEMED CAPTIVATED BY THE BEAST-MAN.

HIS FIRST IMPULSE WAS TO KILL THE CREATURE BUT GREED OUTWEIGHED HIS JEALOUSY.

THIS SPECIMEN OF THE "MISSING LINK" WAS WORTH $100,000 ALIVE!

SUDDENLY, MARSADA HAD AN INSPIRATION. HE'D USE THE GIRL AS "BAIT" TO LURE THE TREE-MAN.

HE SIGNALED HIS COHORTS BACK, AND THE WAY SEEMED CLEAR FOR TARZAN.

THE ENTRANCED GIRL NOTICED NOTHING, BUT TARZAN PERCEIVED MARSADA'S AIM.

THE APE-MAN TURNED, TO SWING UPWARD. MARSADA FEARED HE WOULD ESCAPE ENTIRELY.

EVEN DEAD, THE "MISSING LINK" WAS WORTH A FORTUNE! MARSADA JERKED RIFLE TO SHOULDER.

WHEN TARZAN MOVED, LINDA'S SPELL WAS BROKEN. SHE GLANCED ABOUT HER, AND SAW MARSADA'S PURPOSE.

FORWARD SHE DASHED TO THWART HIM. TOO LATE!

A SHOT RANG OUT. LINDA SCREAMED. TARZAN TUMBLED TO EARTH––– AND LAY STILL! NEXT WEEK: **TRAPPED!**

410- 1-15-39

Tarzan

by Edgar Rice Burroughs

TRAPPED

LINDA CHOKED BACK A SOB OF PITY AS SHE BEHELD THE APE-MAN LYING MOTIONLESS.

SHE DROPPED DOWN BESIDE HIM, AND TO HER RELIEF SHE SAW THAT HE STILL BREATHED.

BUT MARSADA PULLED HER ROUGHLY AWAY, AND SIGNALLED THE BLACKS TO SEIZE THE CAPTIVE.

"WE'VE GOT HIM! WE'VE GOT THE 'MISSING LINK'!" MARSADA CRIED EXCITEDLY.

SO TARZAN WAS BORNE AWAY TO A GREAT CAGE. THE BLACKS THRUST HIM INSIDE AND LOCKED THE DOOR.

SOON HE STIRRED. HIS BULLET-PIERCED HAND THROBBED WITH PAIN. HE LICKED HIS WOUNDS LIKE A BEAST.

SLOWLY CONSCIOUSNESS RETURNED BUT TARZAN WAS STILL DAZED FROM HIS FALL.

HE PERCEIVED ONLY THAT HE WAS IMPRISONED. INSTINCTIVELY HE DASHED AT THE BARS.

FRENZIEDLY HE PULLED AT THEM. FIERCE, ANGRY GROWLS RUMBLED IN HIS THROAT.

THIS WAS NOT TARZAN, THE MAN BUT TARZAN THE JUNGLE BEAST IN ALL FURY.

HOGARTH—

MARSADA LAUGHED. LINDA'S HEART WAS FILLED WITH ACHING SYMPATHY. THE BLACKS SHUDDERED WITH AWE. MIGHTY WAS TARZAN, BUT HIS STRENGTH WAS FUTILE AGAINST THE BARS. HE WAS HOPELESSLY IMPRISONED. NEXT WEEK: A NEW DANGER

411- 1-22-39

Tarzan

by Edgar Rice Burroughs

Copyr. 1939 Edgar Rice Burroughs, Inc.—Trade Mark U.S. Pat.
Off. Produced by Famous Books and Plays—Distribution by
UNITED FEATURE SYNDICATE, Inc.

A NEW DANGER

SEEING TARZAN IMPRISONED, OGLUT, HIS APE-FOE, GRUNTED WITH SATISFACTION, AND HURRIED----

---TO TELL HIS TRIBE THAT THE MAN-THING WHO HAD BEEN THEIR KING WOULD NEVER RETURN.

MEANWHILE TARZAN, STILL DELIRIOUS FROM THE BLOW ON HIS HEAD, GROWLED AND ROARED IN HIS CAGE.

MARSADA WAS ANXIOUS TO TAKE THE 'MISSING LINK' TO JOHN FARR AND COLLECT HIS RICH REWARD.

"THERE'S NO USE CARTING THE CAGE," HE SAID. "WE'LL TIE HIS ARMS AND MARCH HIM UNDER HIS OWN POWER."

HE TURNED TO THE BLACKS AND ORDERED FIVE OF THEM INTO THE CAGE WITH ROPES.

TARZAN SURVEYED THEM WITH THE BLAZING EYES OF A WILD BEAST AT BAY. THEN HE CHARGED.

THE WARRIORS MET HIM CONFIDENTLY. WERE THEY NOT FIVE AGAINST ONE?

THEY DID NOT RECKON, HOWEVER, WITH THE POWER AND FIGHTING SKILL OF THE TREE-CREATURE.

SOON THEY WERE SCREAMING TO BE LET OUT. THE CAGE DOOR WAS OPENED.

TARZAN, TOO, DASHED TOWARD IT. MARSADA LIFTED RIFLE TO KILL HIM, SHOULD HE ESCAPE THE CAGE.

HOGARTH—

BUT THE APE-MAN IN HIS UNREASONING FURY, DID NOT NOTICE THIS NEW PERIL!
NEXT WEEK: BEAST OR MAN?

Tarzan

by Edgar Rice Burroughs

Copt. 1939, Edgar Rice Burroughs, Inc.—"Tarzan" Reg. U.S. Pat.
Off. Registered in Various Parts and Places Throughout the
UNITED FEATURE SYNDICATE, Inc.

MAN OR BEAST?

UNOBSERVED BY THE DAZED, INFURIATED TARZAN, MARSADA STOOD READY TO KILL HIM SHOULD HE ESCAPE.

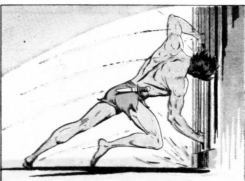

BUT THE BLACKS SLAMMED THE CAGE DOOR AND LOCKED IT. TARZAN WAS SAFE --- FOR A TIME.

"A FEW DAYS IN THE CAGE WILL TAME HIM," MARSADA CHUCKLED. "AND THEN WE'LL GET UNDER WAY."

MEANWHILE LINDA HAD WATCHED THE CAGED CREATURE'S GALLANT FIGHT WITH AWE AND ADMIRATION.

AND NOW SHE SAW THE WOUND IN HIS HAND HAD BEEN RE-OPENED. TOUCHED WITH PITY, SHE HURRIED TO HER TENT AND RETURNED WITH MEDICINE AND BANDAGES.

"DON'T GO NEAR THAT BEAST," MARSADA CRIED, FEARING THE "MISSING LINK" WOULD REACH OUT AND SEIZE HER.

"HE'S NO BEAST," LINDA ANSWERED. "HE'S A MAN --- AND A FINER MAN THAN YOU, GREGOR MARSADA!"

BUT EVEN AS SHE SPOKE SHE WONDERED. WAS THIS CREATURE TRULY A MAN, OR MERELY A MAN-LIKE BEAST?

TARZAN, STILL IN A SPEECHLESS DAZE, STEPPED CLOSE TO THE BARS, DRAWN BY THE MAGNETISM OF HER BEAUTY.

TO THE AMAZEMENT OF THE SPECTATORS HE ANSWERED HER GESTURE BY EXTENDING HIS HAND LIKE AN INJURED CHILD.

HOGARTH—

LINDA'S HAND TOUCHED HIS. HER BLOOD TINGLED. SHE KNEW THAT SHE LOVED HIM!
NEXT WEEK--- THE NET OF DOOM

Tarzan

by EDGAR RICE BURROUGHS

413-2-5-39

THE NET OF DOOM

LOVINGLY, LINDA BANDAGED THE APE-MAN'S HAND WHILE MARSADA WATCHED WITH BITTER JEALOUSY.

THEN SHE TURNED AND WALKED INTO THE FOREST TO BE ALONE WITH HER TORMENTING THOUGHTS.

SHE TOLD HERSELF HOW FOOLISH IT WAS TO FALL IN LOVE WITH THE BEAST MAN, BUT HER HEART WOULD NOT LISTEN.

MEANWHILE TARZAN WAS RECOVERING FROM HIS DAZE, SLOWLY RECALLING THE RECENT RUSH OF EVENTS. HE SMILED.

HOW ABSURD IT WAS TO BE CAGED AS A "MISSING LINK." HE'D ANNOUNCE HIS IDENTITY AND BE SET FREE.

BUT NO! HE REMEMBERED MARSADA'S HATRED OF TARZAN, WHOM HE HAD NEVER CONSCIOUSLY SEEN. IF MARSADA KNEW-----!

TOWARD DUSK, A NATIVE HUNTER, FAR FROM HOME, ASKED BUTANO'S LEAVE TO PASS THE NIGHT IN THE CAMP.

THEN THE HUNTER'S EYES DRIFTED TO THE CAGE. HIS MOUTH FELL AGAPE IN WONDER.

"WHY DO YOU IMPRISON TARZAN?" HE ASKED. "HE IS THE GUARDIAN OF US JUNGLE PEOPLE."

"TARZAN!!!" GASPED BUTANO. "IS THAT TARZAN!" THE HUNTER NODDED.

HOGARTH—

BUTANO HURRIED AWAY TO GIVE THE STARTLING NEWS TO HIS MASTER.

MARSADA'S ASTONISHED EYES BLAZED WITH A MURDEROUS FIRE. "TONIGHT!" HE MURMURED. *NEXT WEEK:* **HELPLESS!**

Tarzan and the Pygmies   103

Tarzan

by EDGAR RICE BURROUGHS

HELPLESS!

WHEN BUTANO REPORTED THAT THEIR CAPTIVE WAS REALLY TARZAN, MARSADA WAS ELATED.

"IF TARZAN DIE," BUTANO GRINNED, "HE NO CAN HELP JUNGLE PEOPLE. WE CAN STEAL IVORY, GOLD."

"HE DIES TONIGHT!" MARSADA WHISPERED HOARSELY.

MEANWHILE, LINDA FARR, UNDER A ROMANTIC SPELL, STROLLED OUT TO GAZE ENRAPTURED AT THE HANDSOME WILD MAN.

UNAWARE THAT HE UNDERSTOOD, SHE POURED OUT HER HEART. "HOW MAGNIFICENT YOU ARE, HOW STRONG, HOW REAL!"

SHE LONGED TO CAST OFF THE FROTH OF CIVILIZATION AND SHARE THE SIMPLE LIFE OF THIS ELEMENTAL MAN.

TARZAN REMAINED SILENT. HE HAD NO WISH TO EMBARRASS THE GIRL, NOR TO REVEAL HIS IDENTITY.

BUT NOW MARSADA CREPT FROM HIS TENT TO FULFILL HIS COWARDLY MISSION. HE HAD ALREADY FRAMED HIS PRETEXT.

HE WOULD SAY THAT HE WAS PASSING THE CAGE, THE WILD MAN CLUTCHED AT HIM, AND HE FIRED IN SELF-DEFENSE.

HE RAISED HIS WEAPON. LINDA SAW HIM. SHE DARTED FROM THE SHADOWS TO STAY THE FATAL SHOT.

SHE LEAPED AT MARSADA, FIGHTING LIKE A TIGRESS TO SAVE THE MAN SHE LOVED.

TARZAN WATCHED HELPLESSLY. THE GIRL WOULD BE OVERWHELMED. THEN MARSADA WOULD FIRE INTO THE CAGE!

NEXT WEEK: **A NEW MENACE**

415-2-19-38

Tarzan

by EDGAR RICE BURROUGHS

A NEW MENACE

LINDA FOUGHT DESPERATELY TO PREVENT MARSADA FROM FIRING INTO THE CAGE. TARZAN WATCHED IN DISMAY. AT ANY MOMENT THE WEAPON MIGHT BE DISCHARGED INTO THE GIRL'S BODY.

ELECTRIFIED BY ALARM, TARZAN PLUNGED AT THE DOOR WITH PRODIGIOUS POWER. THE FASTENINGS CRACKED.

THE APE-MAN LEAPED OUT UPON MARSADA. WRESTING THE GUN FROM HIM, HE FLUNG IT AWAY.

THEN HE LIFTED THE MAN HIGH IN THE AIR AND DASHED HIM TO THE GROUND. MARSADA SCREAMED.

BUTANO HEARD HIS MASTER'S CRY. SCOOPING UP HIS RIFLE, HE RAN TO MARSADA'S AID.

TARZAN SAW HIM COMING. HE TURNED TO ESCAPE IN THE FOREST.

MARSADA, STAGGERING TO HIS FEET, SAW THAT HE HAD MISSED HIS CHERISHED CHANCE TO KILL TARZAN.

NOW ALL HIS VIOLENT WRATH CENTERED ON LINDA. "I'LL GET YOU FOR THIS!" HE SHOUTED.

THE GIRL RAN TO TARZAN, HER ARMS OUTSTRETCHED IN A SILENT PLEA THAT SPOKE PLAINLY: "TAKE ME WITH YOU!"

HOGARTH—

AT THAT MOMENT BUTANO BURST UPON THE SCENE, HIS RIFLE READY FOR ACTION.

"SHOOT!" MARSADA CRIED HYSTERICALLY. "KILL THEM BOTH!"
NEXT WEEK: **FLYING TALONS**

Tarzan

by Edgar Rice Burroughs

FLYING TALONS

AS MARSADA COMMANDED BUTANO TO FIRE, TARZAN PLUNGED FORWARD IN A FLYING LEAP. BUTANO WENT DOWN. THE RIFLE FLEW UP. THE BULLET CRASHED HARMLESSLY INTO THE TREES.

THE APE-MAN WHIRLED TO LINDA. HE KNEW MARSADA WOULD LOOSE HIS VENGEANCE ON HER IF SHE REMAINED.

SO TOSSING HER LIGHTLY TO A SHOULDER, HE SPRANG TREEWARD, AND SPED AWAY INTO THE FOREST.

LINDA CLUNG CLOSE, MORE THRILLED THAN FRIGHTENED BY THE BREATHTAKING FLIGHT.

WHERE HE WAS TAKING HER SHE DID NOT KNOW, NOR DID SHE CARE, SO LONG AS HE REMAINED WITH HER.

WHEN AT LAST THEY HALTED, TARZAN WOVE A BROAD HAMMOCK OF VINES FOR LINDA'S BED.

JUST AS HE STARTED TOWARD A HIGHER BRANCH TO STAND GUARD OVER THE GIRL, HE PAUSED, SNIFFING THE AIR.

HIS EYES DARTED UPWARD----TO MEET THE FIERCE FLASHING EYES OF A LEOPARD!

LINDA GLANCED UP TOO. SHE SCREAMED. THE GREAT CAT, EXCITED BY HER CRY, SPRANG AT HER.

IN A FLASH, TARZAN SHOVED HER ASIDE----- AND HIMSELF RECEIVED THE FULL FORCE OF THE LEOPARD'S PLUNGE.

TOGETHER THEY TUMBLED EARTHWARD, BEAST AND BEAST-MAN, IN A TANGLE OF TALONS AND HUMAN FLESH!
NEXT WEEK:
BROKEN PARADISE

HOGARTH—

417-3-5-39

Tarzan

by EDGAR RICE BURROUGHS

BROKEN PARADISE

WHEN THE PLUNGING LEOPARD STRUCK TARZAN, BOTH TUMBLED TO EARTH IN A TANGLE OF SAVAGE FURY.

THOUGH THE BEAST CUSHIONED TARZAN'S FALL, IT DID NOT LOOSEN ITS STRONG EMBRACE.

LOOKING DOWN, LINDA WAS TERRIFIED, FOR SHE WAS CERTAIN HER BELOVED DEFENDER WOULD DIE.

BUT NOW SHE SAW HIS ARM WHIP AROUND THE LEOPARD'S NECK AND THROTTLE THE STRUGGLING BEAST.

HE ASCENDED THEN TO THE ASTONISHED, TREMBLING GIRL WHO FOUND COMFORT IN HIS NEARNESS.

THE DAYS THAT FOLLOWED WERE FOR LINDA A JUNGLE IDYLL. SHE EXULTED IN THE FREEDOM OF THE PRIMITIVE WORLD.

SHE DELIGHTED IN THE SOCIETY OF JUNGLE CREATURES TO WHICH HER COMPANION INTRODUCED HER.

UNAWARE THAT HE UNDERSTOOD, SHE OFTEN DECLARED HER LOVE FOR THE STALWART TREE-MAN.

TARZAN GAVE NO SIGN OF COMPREHENSION. HE HAD NO WISH TO EMBARRASS HER, NOR TO DISTURB HER EASY COMRADESHIP.

BUT THEIR IDYLL ENDED ABRUPTLY. ONE DAY WHILE THEY FROLICKED IN A CRYSTAL POOL, TARZAN LOOKED UP---- TO SEE THE POOL SURROUNDED BY A HORDE OF APES, WHOSE EVERY ACTION INDICATED HOSTILITY.

HOGARTH—

THEIR BLOODSHOT EYES FOCUSED ON LINDA, AND THEIR LIPS MUMBLED THE AWFUL "DUM-DUM!"—THE DANCE OF DEATH!

NEXT WEEK-- CAPTURED

418-3-12-39

Tarzan

by Edgar Rice Burroughs

CAPTURED

TARZAN AND LINDA WERE TRAPPED BY THE HOSTILE APES, NOR COULD TARZAN PERCEIVE ANY MEANS OF ESCAPE.

BRANCHES OVERHUNG THE POOL, BUT EVEN THE MIGHTY JUNGLE LORD COULD NOT SPRING FROM THE WATER.

SO, WITH THE TERRIFIED LINDA, HE SUBMITTED TO THE ENEMY, WHO TOOK THEM TO THE SITE OF THE DUM-DUM.

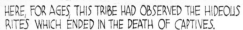

HERE, FOR AGES, THIS TRIBE HAD OBSERVED THE HIDEOUS RITES WHICH ENDED IN THE DEATH OF CAPTIVES.

TARZAN COULD HAVE BROKEN AWAY FROM HIS CAPTORS, BUT HE WOULD NOT ESCAPE WITHOUT THE GIRL.

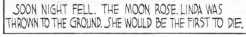

SOON NIGHT FELL. THE MOON ROSE. LINDA WAS THROWN TO THE GROUND. SHE WOULD BE THE FIRST TO DIE.

THE EARTHDRUM BOOMED ITS WEIRD PRELUDE TO DEATH. THE APES WERE SEIZED WITH FRENZY.

THIS WAS THE MOMENT TARZAN WAS AWAITING, WHEN THE DULL MINDS OF HIS CAPTORS WOULD BE CONFUSED.

"I AM TARZAN, KING AMONG APES," HE ROARED. "YOU CANNOT KILL TARZAN! YOU CANNOT KILL TARZAN'S SHE!"

THE APES WERE BEWILDERED BY THE MAN-THING WHO SPOKE THEIR LANGUAGE. BUT ONE LUMBERED FORWARD.

HOGARTH—

NEXT WEEK: FRIEND AND FOE

"I BAK-DAK," HE SNARLED. "BAK-DAK KING HERE. BAK-DAK KILL TARZAN—KILL TARZAN'S SHE!" THE JUNGLE LORD GROWLED. "BAK-DAK KING NOW. BAK-DAK NOT BE KING LONG. TARZAN KILL!"

Tarzan

by EDGAR RICE BURROUGHS

Copr. 1938 Edgar Rice Burroughs, Inc.—Tm Reg. U. S. Pat.
Off. Produced by Famous Books and Plays Distributed by
UNITED FEATURE SYNDICATE, Inc.

FRIEND AND FOE

TARZAN AND BAK-DAK MET IN FURIOUS COMBAT, TO BATTLE UNTIL ONE SHOULD DIE.

LINDA WAS ASTONISHED AND TERRIFIED. FIRST SHE HAD HEARD HER TREE-MAN CONVERSING WITH THE APES.

AND NOW, AS HE FOUGHT, HE GROWLED LIKE A BEAST. WAS HE, AFTER ALL, AKIN TO THESE CREATURES?

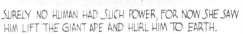

SURELY NO HUMAN HAD SUCH POWER, FOR NOW SHE SAW HIM LIFT THE GIANT APE AND HURL HIM TO EARTH.

THE APE-KING TRIED TO RISE, BUT HE FELL BACK SCREAMING WITH PAIN. HIS LEG WAS BROKEN.

TARZAN ADVANCED. THE APES BELIEVED HE WOULD KILL HIS ANTAGONIST, AS WAS HIS RIGHT.

BUT THE JUNGLE LORD STOOPED AND FELT THE INJURY. THEN HE VANISHED INTO THE FOREST.

SOON HE RETURNED WITH BRANCHES AND VINES, AND BOUND THEM AS A SPLINT ON A WOUNDED LEG.

THEN HE SAID: "WHEN GORO THE MOON COMES TWICE FULL, BAK-DAK WILL WALK AS BEFORE."

THE APES KNEW LITTLE OF SENTIMENT, BUT GRUFF OLD BAK-DAK FELT A CERTAIN VAGUE GRATITUDE TARZAN'S VICTORY MADE HIM KING— —AND THE TRIBE WAS PLEASED TO HAVE A MONARCH SO STRONG AND WISE.

NEXT WEEK: **THE HALF-MEN**

BUT HIS PERIL WAS NOT PAST, FOR GREGOR MARSADA LINGERED IN THE JUNGLE, DETERMINED TO HUNT HIM DOWN!

420-3-26-39

Tarzan

by Edgar Rice Burroughs

THE HALF-MEN

ONE DAY WHEN MARSADA WAS HUNTING TARZAN, A BAND OF MONSTROUS CREATURES SPRANG FROM AMBUSH. HE FIRED. ONE FELL. BUT OTHERS WERE ALREADY UPON HIM.

THEN MARSADA WAS TAKEN BY THESE GROTESQUE HALF-MEN TO THE CAVERN-LAIR OF MAL-YUT, THEIR CHIEF.

TO MAL-YUT THEY GAVE THE REVOLVER, DESCRIBING ITS DEADLY MAGIC. HE FINGERED IT CURIOUSLY.

BY ACCIDENT HE DISCHARGED THE GUN. ONE OF THE HALF-MEN SCREAMED AND FELL. MAL-YUT LAUGHED.

AGAIN AND AGAIN HE FIRED, AMUSED BY THE DEATH-DEALING MAGIC, UNTIL THE REVOLVER WAS EMPTY.

THEN DEMANDING THAT THE MYSTIC POWER BE RESTORED, HE GAVE THE GUN EAGERLY, TRUSTFULLY TO MARSADA.

THE STRANGER RELOADED IT— AND FIRED! THE BULLET WHISTLED NEAR THE TERRIFIED CHIEF— MARSADA SMILED.

HE HAD NO WISH TO KILL—— FOR ALREADY HE WAS SCHEMING TO USE THESE MONSTERS FOR HIS EVIL PURPOSE.

MEANWHILE TARZAN, AS THE NEW KING, INQUIRED OF HIS APES WHO THEIR ENEMIES WERE.

"LINGOOS," ONE REPLIED. "ARE THE LINGOOS MEN?" HE ASKED. SOME OF THE APES SAID YES—SOME SAID NO.

NEXT WEEK: THE FOE DRAWS —NEAR—

HOGARTH—

"ARE THEY APES?" SOME SAID YES— SOME SAID NO; BUT THE EYES OF ALL WERE FILLED WITH TERROR!

421-4-2-39

Tarzan

by EDGAR RICE BURROUGHS

THE FOE DRAWS NEAR

Copyr. 1939 Edgar Rice Burroughs, Inc.—Tm. Reg. U.S. Pat. Off. and in Foreign Mtes. and Also Protected by UNITED FEATURE SYNDICATE, Inc.

MAL-YUT, CHIEF OF THE HALF-MEN, WAS AWED BY THE DEADLY MAGIC OF MARSADA'S THUNDER-STICK.

WITH ANIMAL CUNNING AND HUMAN CRAFTINESS HE DECIDED TO MAKE THIS WIZARD HIS FRIEND. MARSADA WAS DELIGHTED. HE COULD TRAIN THESE FIERCE CREATURES TO RAID NATIVE VILLAGES FOR IVORY.

BUT FIRST HE MUST DESTROY THE ONLY OBSTACLE TO HIS PLAN—TARZAN, THE JUNGLE GUARDIAN.

TARZAN AND LINDA DWELT NOW WITH THE APE-TRIBE, OF WHICH TARZAN HAD BECOME KING.

THE GIRL FELT SECURE WITH SO MANY STRONG PROTECTORS. BUT TARZAN WAS NOT SO CERTAIN OF SECURITY.

HE WAS PUZZLED BY THE LINGOOS, THE MYSTERIOUS CREATURES WHO WERE ENEMIES OF THE TRIBE.

THROUGH THE LONG DAYS BAK-DAK SAT UNDER A TREE, HIS BROKEN LEG BOUND IN A SPLINT TARZAN MADE.

BAK-DAK FRETTED FOR FEAR THE LINGOOS WOULD COME, AND HE WOULD BE HELPLESS TO ESCAPE.

SO TARZAN CARVED CRUDE CRUTCHES AND TAUGHT HIM TO WALK ON THEM, WHILE THE TRIBE MARVELED.

ONE DAY TARZAN CAUGHT A STRANGE SCENT, A SCENT NEITHER HUMAN NOR ANIMAL, YET SOMEWHAT BOTH.

THE SCENT GREW STRONGER. THE APES CAUGHT IT TOO. "LINGOOS!" THEY CRIED IN DISMAY. *NEXT WEEK:* **THE LINGOOS ATTACK**

Tarzan
by Edgar Rice Burroughs

Copr. 1936, Edgar Rice Burroughs, Inc. — Tm. Reg. U. S. Pat.
Off. "Man"-and by Famous Books and Plays. Distributed by
UNITED FEATURE SYNDICATE, Inc.

THE LINGOOS ATTACK

422- 4-9-39

"LINGOOS! LINGOOS!" SHRIEKED THE APES, AND SOON THE CLEARING SWARMED WITH THE FRIGHTFUL HALF-MEN.

AS THE KING OF THE TRIBE, IT WAS TARZAN'S DUTY TO DIRECT THE DEFENSE BUT THERE WAS NO DEFENSE.

THE APES, USUALLY FIERCE AND FEARLESS, WERE FLEEING IN CONFUSION.

"STAND AND FIGHT!" TARZAN SHOUTED FOR HE SAW THEY WERE SURROUNDED. THEY MUST FIGHT OR YIELD.

THE APES, THOUGH PANIC STRICKEN, WERE SHOCKED INTO OBEDIENCE BY THE SHARP COMMAND.

AND NOW THE APE-MAN RANGED HIS FIGHTING BEASTS INTO A TIGHT CIRCLE AROUND LINDA.

AND HE HIMSELF SET THE EXAMPLE OF HEROIC, EFFECTIVE COMBAT.

THE LINGOOS WERE ASTONISHED ALWAYS THEY HAD CONQUERED AND ENSLAVED THE APES WITH SMALL EFFORT

THEY SAW THE MAN-APE WAS THE INSPIRATION OF THIS NEW RESISTANCE.

HOGARTH—

SO SWINGING STONE HATCHETS, THRUSTING STONE-TIPPED SPEARS, THEY CENTERED THEIR ATTACK ON TARZAN. THE APES RALLIED AROUND HIM, FIGHTING NOW WITH RECKLESS FURY.

BUT THE SUPERIOR WEAPONS OF THE LINGOOS WERE WRITING IN BLOOD A PROPHECY OF THEIR VICTORY.
NEXT WEEK: BAK-DAK'S SACRIFICE

Tarzan

by EDGAR RICE BURROUGHS

BAK-DAK'S SACRIFICE

THE TEEMING LINGOOS SOUGHT TO ISOLATE TARZAN AND CENTER THEIR ATTACK ON HIM.

MEANWHILE, THE CRIPPLED BAK-DAK LOOKED ON, POWERLESS TO AID, AND IGNORED BY THE LINGOOS AS HARMLESS. BUT WHEN HE SAW TARZAN SO GRIEVOUSLY MENACED, HE HOBBLED FORWARD ON THE CRUTCHES TARZAN HAD MADE.

A LINGOO TRIED TO HALT HIM. BAK-DAK STRUCK WITH A CRUTCH. HIS ASSAILANT FELL. THE CRUTCH BROKE.

AND NOW BAK-DAK SAW TARZAN ATTACKED FROM BEHIND. HE HURLED HIS REMAINING CRUTCH.

THE MISSILE FOUND ITS MARK. THE ATTACKER DROPPED. THE APE-MAN WAS SAVED—FOR A TIME AT LEAST.

THEN BAK-DAK LIMPED HEROICALLY INTO BATTLE, THOUGH HIS BROKEN LEG WAS GRINDING AND THROBBING WITH PAIN.

"GO, TARZAN! YOU STAY, YOU DIE!" HE SAID. TARZAN TOO REALIZED THAT DEATH OR CAPTURE WAS INEVITABLE.

FOR HIMSELF HE DID NOT CARE—BUT WHAT OF LINDA? SUDDENLY HE WHIRLED AND SEIZED HER.

THEN, WITH BAK-DAK AT HIS SIDE, HE FOUGHT HIS WAY TO THE EDGE OF THE CLEARING.

INTO THE TREES HE SPRANG. TO HIS SURPRISE, A BAND OF LINGOOS SWARMED AFTER HIM.

THEY TOO WERE TREE CREATURES, AND NO BURDEN IMPEDED THEIR SWIFT PURSUIT.

NEXT WEEK: CAPTURED!

Tarzan

CAPTURED!

by EDGAR RICE BURROUGHS

Copr 1939 Edgar Rice Burroughs, Inc —Tm Reg U S Pat.
Off. Produced in Picture Books and Plays Distributed by
UNITED FEATURE SYNDICATE, Inc

THROUGH THE TREES TARZAN FLEW WITH LINDA, WHILE THE DREADFUL LINGOOS SWEPT AROUND HIM.

HE TRIED TO FILTER THROUGH THE SWARM, AND HE HAD ALMOST SUCCEEDED WHEN ONE OF THE HALF-MEN DIVED RECKLESSLY UPON HIM AND TOPPLED HIM FROM A BOUGH.

AS HE FELL, TARZAN HUGGED LINDA CLOSE, TO SHIELD HER FROM THE SCRAPING BRANCHES.

WHEN THEY STRUCK THE GROUND, LINGOOS PILED UPON THEM AND TOOK THEM PRISONER.

AND NOW MARSADA EMERGED FROM THE FOREST, WHERE HE HAD HIDDEN DURING THE BATTLE

"THESE ARE MY CREATURES," HE BOASTED, INDICATING THE LINGOOS, "AND THEY DO MY BIDDING."

IGNORING TARZAN, HE PUT AN ARM AROUND LINDA, AND GLOATED: "NOW YOU ARE UNDER MY COMMAND."

LINDA STRUGGLED, BUT THE RUFFIAN ONLY DREW HER CLOSER. A RARE ANGER ROSE IN THE HEART OF TARZAN.

HE WRENCHED LOOSE FROM HIS CAPTORS, CLUTCHED MARSADA, AND HURLED HIM TO THE GROUND.

BUT THE LINGOOS QUICKLY SEIZED HIM AGAIN.

MARSADA LOOKED UP AT LINDA AND SCOWLED: "YOUR APISH BOY FRIEND WON'T COME BETWEEN US AGAIN FOR SOON HE SHALL DIE!"

HOGARTH—

NEXT WEEK: **DANGEROUS MERCY**

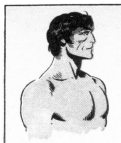

Tarzan

by Edgar Rice Burroughs

Copr. 1939 Edgar Rice Burroughs, Inc.—Reg. U.S. Pat.
Off. Produced by Famous Books and Plays. Distributed by
UNITED FEATURE SYNDICATE, Inc.

125-4-30-39

DANGEROUS MERCY

MARSADA WAS TEMPTED TO ORDER TARZAN SLAIN, BUT HE WANTED TO EXHIBIT HIS PRIZE TO MAL-YLIT.

SO NOW HE WALKED AHEAD WITH LINDA, WHILE TARZAN WAS HERDED WITH THE CAPTIVE BEASTS.

THE LINGOOS STRUTTED, DISPLAYING ARROGANTLY THEIR "ARMED POWER" OVER THE "BACKWARD" APES.

WHEN THE PRISONERS WERE LINKED BY A GRASS ROPE, TARZAN WAS PLACED BEHIND BAK-DAK, THE CRIPPLE.

"MARCH!" A LINGOO ORDERED. BAK-DAK HOBBLED FORWARD, HIS FACE WRITHING IN PAIN, WHILE HIS CAPTORS LAUGHED AT HIS GROTESQUE GAIT.

FINALLY THE POOR BEAST COLLAPSED. THE GUARD RAINED BLOWS ON HIM, COMMANDING HIM TO RISE.

TARZAN WAS AROUSED BY SUCH WANTON, HUMAN CRUELTY- A VICE UNKNOWN TO BEASTS.

HIS ANGER BURST THE BONDS OF CAUTION. HE SWUNG A PUNISHING BLOW. THE GUARD FELL SENSELESS.

THE LINGOOS COWERED, FOR THEY WERE IMPRESSED BY FORCE AND MASTERY

SO, UNHINDERED, TARZAN LIFTED UP THE PITIFUL APE, AND SUPPORTED HIM ON THE MARCH.

THUS THEY CAME TO THE CAVE OF MAL-YLIT. THE LINGOO CHIEF GAZED CURIOUSLY AT LINDA. THEN MARSADA SPOKE UP QUICKLY: "SHE SHALL BE MY SLAVE!"

NEXT WEEK: CRISIS

HOGARTH-

Tarzan

by EDGAR RICE BURROUGHS

CRISIS

THE WORDS BURNED HOT IN TARZAN'S BRAIN AS MARSADA REPEATED, "SHE SHALL BE MY SLAVE."

MAL-YUT YIELDED, FOR HE FEARED THE WRATH OF THE WHITE WIZARD. "SHE SHALL BE YOUR SLAVE," HE MUTTERED.

MARSADA TOOK LINDA'S ARM, AND CAST A GLANCE OF TRIUMPH AT TARAN.

THE APE-MAN LOOKED ABOUT HIM ESTIMATING THE CHANCES OF ESCAPING WITH THE GIRL. HOPELESS!

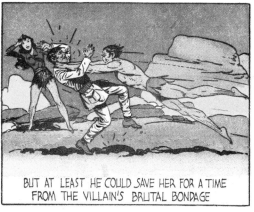

BUT AT LEAST HE COULD SAVE HER FOR A TIME FROM THE VILLAIN'S BRUTAL BONDAGE

SUDDENLY TARZAN LEAPED AT MARSADA, SEIZED HIM, LIFTED HIM HIGH, AND DASHED HIM TO THE GROUND.

CRACKING BONES PROCLAIMED THAT THE SCOUNDREL WOULD BE HELPLESS FOR WEEKS.

BUT NOW THE GUARDS SPRANG AT TARZAN TO SUBDUE HIM—TO KILL HIM IF NEED BE.

FRANTIC WITH FEAR FOR THE MAN SHE LOVED, LINDA GRASPED THE REVOLVER THAT LAY NEAR MAL-YUT.

AIMING AT A LINGOO WHO THREATENED TARZAN FROM BEHIND SHE PULLED THE TRIGGER.

ONLY A DULL CLICK REWARDED HER DESPERATE ATTEMPT. THE GUN WAS EMPTY!

THEN THE GUARD STRUCK TARZAN. HE SLUMPED TO THE GROUND, AND LAY STILL.

NEXT WEEK: **THE HATCHET-DEATH**

Tarzan
by EDGAR RICE BURROUGHS

THE HATCHET DEATH

TARZAN WAS ONLY STUNNED BY THE LINGOO'S BLOW, AND MAL-YUT ORDERED HIM AND LINDA TO THE PRISON CAVE.

THERE THE GIRL RIPPED PIECES FROM HER TATTERED GARMENTS AND BOUND UP HIS HEAD.

WHILE THE WOUND WAS HEALING, TARZAN STUDIED MEANS OF ESCAPE.

ONE DAY HE LED HIS FELLOW CAPTIVES IN A DESPERATE BREAK FOR FREEDOM, BUT THE LINGOOS OVERWHELMED HIM.

"THIS TARZAN IS TOO DANGEROUS," MAL-YUT CONCLUDED. "LET HIM DIE THE HATCHET DEATH."

SO THE APE-MAN WAS BROUGHT TO A GREAT CLEARING FRINGED WITH LINGOO WARRIORS.

HERE HE WAS UNBOUND AND STATIONED BEFORE A GIANT TREE. IN FRONT OF HIM, LINGOO WARRIORS FORMED IN LINE. THE FIRST HURLED A STONE HATCHET.

TARZAN DODGED EASILY. THE BLADE SANK INTO THE TREE. THEN ANOTHER AND ANOTHER.

BUT THESE WERE THE NOVICE HURLERS. NOW A TEAM OF CHAMPIONS STEPPED FORWARD.

IN DIZZY SUCCESSION, THE KEEN-EDGED MISSILES WHIZZED CLOSE. TARZAN WAS IN PERIL OF HIS LIFE!

AND FROM A TREE AT THE JUNGLE'S EDGE, A REMARKABLE CREATURE LOOKED DOWN ON THE STIRRING DRAMA.

NEXT WEEK: THE MYSTERIOUS SPECTATOR

HOGARTH—

Tarzan

by EDGAR RICE BURROUGHS — THE MYSTERIOUS SPECTATOR

428-5-21-39

THE TREE-WOMAN GAZED SPELL-BOUND AT THE HANDSOME STRANGER WHO WAS IMPERILLED BY THE HALF-MEN.

SUDDENLY SHE WHIRLED AND SPED AWAY THROUGH THE BRANCHES WITH THE GRACE AND AGILITY OF TARZAN HIMSELF.

MEANWHILE, THE HATCHET-HURLERS CONTINUED WITH THEIR MURDEROUS GAME, WITH THE APE-MAN AS A LIVING TARGET.

ONE OF THE MISSILES GRAZED HIS ARM AND DREW BLOOD. THE LINGOOS SHOUTED WITH GLEE.

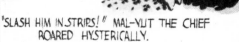

"SLASH HIM IN STRIPS!" MAL-YUT THE CHIEF ROARED HYSTERICALLY.

ONE TEAM OF HATCHET THROWERS SUCCEEDED ANOTHER, EACH MORE SKILLFUL THAN THE LAST.

MARSADA HOBBLED ABOUT EXCITEDLY. THIS WAS SURELY THE END OF HIS FOE.

LINDA TREMBLED WITH FEAR, FOR THE MAN SHE LOVED—AND FOR HERSELF WHEN HE SHOULD DIE.

BUT TARZAN TURNED SWIFTLY AND PULLED OUT SEVERAL HATCHETS WHICH HAD STUCK IN THE TREE.

AND HE RAINED THEM AT THE HURLERS WITH DEADLY ACCURACY.

THE LINGOOS ABANDONED THEIR ORDERLY CONTEST. THEY MUST KILL THIS DANGEROUS CAPTIVE AT ONCE.

HOGARTH—

SO NOW A RIOTOUS VOLLEY OF SPEARS AND HATCHETS WHIRLED TOWARD TARZAN!
NEXT WEEK: **KULEEAH, THE TREE-WOMAN**

Tarzan

by Edgar Rice Burroughs

KULEEAH
THE TREE-WOMAN

TO ESCAPE THE DEADLY MISSILES OF HIS FOES, TARZAN THREW HIMSELF QUICKLY UPON THE GROUND.

FROM EVERY QUARTER LINGOOS RAN TOWARD HIM, EAGER TO DELIVER THE STROKE OF DEATH.

MEANWHILE, AT THE FOREST'S EDGE, A LEGION OF MYSTERIOUS TREE-WOMEN DROPPED TO EARTH.

WITH SPIRITED CRIES THEY ASSAILED THE HALF-MEN, MANY OF WHOM TURNED TO MEET THIS NEW MENACE.

WITH GAY ENTHUSIASM THEY BATTLED THEIR WAY TO TARZAN, WHO WAS ENGAGED WITH A LINGOO BAND.

"LET US BEAR AWAY THE STRANGERS," SHOUTED KULEEAH, CHIEF OF THE AMAZONS; "THE HANDSOME ONE IS MINE!"

THE APE-MAN HAD NO TIME TO WONDER WHO OR WHAT SHE WAS, BUT HE RECOGNIZED IN HER A REMARKABLE ALLY. AS THEY FOUGHT SIDE BY SIDE, HE MARVELED AT HER STRENGTH AND SPARKLING COURAGE.

AND NOW AND THEN KULEEAH CAST A GLANCE OF FRANK APPROVAL AT THE MIGHTY JUNGLE LORD.

SUDDENLY TARZAN WAS STRUCK FROM BEHIND. HE FELL UNCONSCIOUS. KULEEAH SWOOPED DOWN----

...GATHERED HIM IN HER ARMS, AND DASHED THROUGH THE RANKS OF THE BEWILDERED HALF-MEN.

THEN BEARING HER PRECIOUS BURDEN, SHE LEAPED INTO THE TREES, AND VANISHED.

HOGARTH—
NEXT WEEK: *CAPTIVE HUSBANDS*

Tarzan

by Edgar Rice Burroughs

CAPTIVE HUSBANDS

WITH AGILE EASE THE POWERFUL KULEEAH BORE THE UNCONSCIOUS TARZAN THROUGH THE TREES.

NOW AND THEN SHE HALTED, KISSED HIM TENDERLY, THEN RESUMED HER DIZZY FLIGHT.

BEHIND SWARMED THE OTHER TREE-WOMEN, BEARING LINDA AND MARSADA.

SOON THEY APPROACHED A REMARKABLE VILLAGE BUILT HIGH IN THE TREES.

TO A LARGE HUT KULEEAH TOOK TARZAN. HE OPENED HIS EYES SLOWLY AND LOOKED ABOUT HIM.

THREE FRAIL, DOCILE MEN SCURRIED ABOUT AT KULEEAH'S SHARP COMMANDS.

THESE, TARZAN JUDGED, WERE HER HUSBANDS, AND NOW APPARENTLY HE HAD BEEN ADDED TO HER HOUSEHOLD.

WHEN KULEEAH LEFT, TARZAN QUESTIONED THEM, FOR THEIR LANGUAGE WAS AKIN TO THAT OF THE GREAT APES.

"MEN ARE PRISONERS HERE," SAID ONE, "FOR IN OUR SPECIES ONLY THE WOMEN CAN TRAVEL THROUGH THE TREES."

UNITED FEATURE SYNDICATE

"AND YOU WILL REMAIN HERE UNTIL YOU DIE," SAID ANOTHER. TARZAN SMILED.

HE STEPPED TO THE BALCONY TO SURVEY THE STRANGE ARBOREAL VILLAGE.

NEXT WEEK: CONQUERING AMAZON

AND HE HEARD KULEEAH BOASTING: "SEE WHAT A FINE NEW HUSBAND I HAVE CAPTURED!"

HOGARTH—

Tarzan

by Edgar Rice Burroughs

431-6-11-39

CONQUERING AMAZON

KULEEAH ROAMED THE ARBOREAL VILLAGE, BOASTING OF TARZAN AS HER NEW SLAVE-HUSBAND.

MARSADA WATCHED BITTERLY. NO ONE HAD CLAIMED HIM FOR A HUSBAND, FOR HE WAS WEAK AND CRIPPLED.

NEARBY, HE SAW A SPEAR---HERE WAS HIS CHANCE TO TAKE FINAL REVENGE ON THE HATED TARZAN.

THE APE-MAN SPIED HIM AND MADE READY TO DODGE. KULEEAH SAW HIM TOO. SHE LEAPED DOWN UPON HIM.

FURIOUSLY SHE SEIZED MARSADA AND HURLED HIM TO INSTANT DEATH ON THE GROUND BELOW.

THEN SHE SWUNG TO TARZAN'S SIDE. "I SAVED YOUR LIFE. NOW YOU WILL LOVE ME," SHE SAID JAUNTILY.

"LOVE CANNOT BE COMMANDED," THE APE-MAN REPLIED WITH AN AMUSED SMILE.

THE OTHER AMAZONS HOWLED WITH GLEE, FOR THEY ENJOYED THE EMBARRASSMENT OF IMPERIOUS KULEEAH.

"I WILL MAKE YOU LOVE ME," SHE CRIED ANGRILY. "I AM STRONG. YOU SAW ---I CONQUERED A MAN!"

"HE WAS WEAK AND CRIPPLED," TARZAN TAUNTED. AGAIN THE WARRIOR WOMEN HOOTED AT KULEEAH.

HOGARTH—

"YOU HAVE CAPTURED HIM, BUT HE IS MASTER," THEY SHOUTED.

NEXT WEEK: THE DUEL

"I CAN CONQUER ANY MAN," CRIED THE WILD-HEARTED KULEEAH. "HE WILL LOVE ME—OR DIE!"

Tarzan

by Edgar Rice Burroughs

THE DUEL

152-6-18-39

"LOVE ME OR DIE!" KULEEAH SCREAMED, PRESSING THE SPEAR AGAINST TARZAN'S BREAST.

"NO!" SHOUTED AN AMAZON, "YOU CANNOT COMMAND HIM UNTIL YOU'VE CONQUERED HIM IN A FAIR DUEL."----"FIGHT! FIGHT!" CRIED AN EXCITED CHORUS. "VERY WELL, I'LL FIGHT---AND CONQUER," KULEEAH BOASTED.

THEN SHE SEIZED TARZAN AND DROPPED DOWN THROUGH THE TREES. HE OFFERED NO RESISTANCE.

GLEEFULLY THE TREE-WOMEN ROMPED DOWN TO WITNESS THE CONFLICT.

A WOMAN WARRIOR BROUGHT TARZAN A BUNDLE OF CLUBS. "CHOOSE ONE," SHE DIRECTED.

"AND CHOOSE WISELY," SAID ANOTHER, "FOR KULEEAH IS THE MIGHTIEST OF OUR MIGHTY RACE."

TARZAN TOOK THE SMALLEST CLUB. KULEEAH FUMED AT THIS GESTURE OF SCORN--AND TOOK THE LARGEST CLUB.

AT A SIGNAL, WILD KULEEAH RUSHED AT TARZAN. WHEN SHE CAME CLOSE, HE FLUNG HIS CLUB ASIDE.

THEN HE SEIZED HER WRIST, WHIRLED, AND TOSSED HER GENTLY OVER A SHOULDER.

THE AMAZONS SHRIEKED WITH LAUGHTER. KULEEAH ROSE UP RAGING. BEFORE, SHE HAD PLANNED TO DISARM OR STUN HER OPPONENT, BUT NOW----

NEXT WEEK: A WOMAN SCORNED

HOGARTH

---SHE MEANT TO KILL HIM---BY FAIR MEANS OR FOUL!

Tarzan
by EDGAR RICE BURROUGHS

Copr. 1939, Edgar Rice Burroughs, Inc.—Tm. Reg. U.S. Pat.
Off. Produced by Famous Books and Plays. Distributed by
UNITED FEATURE SYNDICATE, Inc.

A WOMAN SCORNED

THE PROUD KULEEAH WAS FURIOUS BECAUSE TARZAN HAD MADE SPORT OF HER. NOW SHE DASHED TOWARD HIM, DETERMINED TO REDEEM HER PRIDE WITH HIS BLOOD.

SHE AIMED A MURDEROUS BLOW AT THE HEAD OF THE UNARMED APE-MAN.

AGAIN TARZAN DODGED, WHIRLED, SEIZED HER, AND LIFTED HER HIGH ABOVE HIS HEAD.

THERE HE HELD HER, KICKING AND SQUIRMING WHILE HER COMRADES HURLED GLEEFUL TAUNTS.

THOUGH THEY LAUGHED AT KULEEAH'S PLIGHT, THEY WERE IMPRESSED BY THE MIGHTY TARZAN.

"HE CAN BE MY HUSBAND, THOUGH HE CONQUER ME AND RULE MY HUT," CRIED ONE.

THIS WAS HERESY AMONG THE AMAZONS, WHO PRIDED THEMSELVES ON THEIR DOMINANCE OVER MEN.

"I'LL TAKE HIM," SHOUTED ANOTHER. "NO, HE'S MINE," INSISTED A THIRD. SOON THE TRIBE WAS IN TURMOIL.

AS THE WARRIOR WOMEN FOUGHT AMONG THEMSELVES, TARZAN SET KULEEAH DOWN.

SHE RAN AWAY TO GET HER BOW AND ARROWS. IF SHE COULD NOT HAVE HIM, NO OTHER WOULD.

THEN, SUDDENLY, INTO THIS WILD CONFUSION BURST A PACK OF HUNGRY LIONS!
NEXT WEEK: **LIFE FOR DEATH**

A34-7-2-39

Tarzan

by EDGAR RICE BURROUGHS

LIFE FOR DEATH

"LIONS! LIONS!" THE FRANTIC CRY RANG THROUGH THE FOREST, AND THE AMAZONS FLED IN PANIC.

FORGOTTEN WAS TARZAN, AS THEY RACED TO THE EDGE OF THE CLEARING AND SPRANG INTO THE TREES.

KULEEAH, HOWEVER, STUMBLED AND FELL, AND A LION RACED TOWARD HER TO CLAIM ITS PREY.

TARZAN LEAPED FORWARD TO SAVE HER. THOUGH SHE HAD TRIED TO KILL HIM, HE BORE HER NO ILL-WILL.

THESE WILD WOMEN OF THE FOREST, HE CONCLUDED, WERE NO MORE ACCOUNTABLE THAN THEIR CIVILIZED SISTERS.

AS TARZAN REACHED HER, KULEEAH WAS RISING, AND THE LION WAS REARING UP TO LOCK HER IN FATAL EMBRACE.

LIKE A FLASH, TARZAN SHOVED HER ASIDE AND TOOK HER PLACE IN THE SHADOW OF DEATH.

THE BEAST LUNGED FORWARD. THE APE-MAN DUCKED BENEATH ITS FORELEGS.

AT THE SAME TIME HIS KNIFE PLUNGED DEEP INTO THE CARNIVORE'S SIDE. IT FELL.

TARZAN TURNED SWIFTLY TO KULEEAH, WHO STOOD DAZED AND FROZEN WITH ASTONISHMENT.

HE SWEPT HER UP IN HIS ARMS AND STARTED TO RUN.

NEXT WEEK: A DANGEROUS TURN

HOGARTH—

BUT ANOTHER LION DASHED UP FROM THE SIDE. ITS FURIOUS CHARGE TOPPLED TARZAN TO THE GROUND!

Tarzan

by Edgar Rice Burroughs

Copr. 1939, Edgar Rice Burroughs, Inc.—Tm. Reg. U.S. Pat.
Off. Produced by Famous Books and Plays. Distributed by
UNITED FEATURE SYNDICATE, Inc.

A DANGEROUS TURN

AS THE CHARGING LION SIDESWIPED HIM, TARZAN FELL. HIS HEAD STRUCK A ROCK AND HE LAY STILL.

THE BEAST WAS CARRIED PAST BY HIS OWN MOMENTUM, BUT SWIFTLY HE WHIRLED TO RENEW THE CHARGE.

ELECTRIFIED BY TARZAN'S PERIL, KULEEAH SCOOPED HIM UP AND FLED INTO THE TREES.

ON THE BALCONY OF HER HUT SHE HELD HIM CLOSE AND KISSED HIM.

FORGOTTEN NOW WAS THEIR CONFLICT. SHE BELIEVED HIS ATTEMPT TO SAVE HER FROM THE LION WAS A SIGN THAT HE REALLY LOVED HER.

AS TARZAN WAS RECOVERING FROM HIS DAZE, HE SAW THE OTHER WARRIOR WOMEN HOVERING ABOUT, SCOWLING JEALOUSLY.

"HE IS NOT YOURS, KULEEAH," SAID ONE. "BECAUSE YOU FAILED TO CONQUER HIM."

"I WANT HIM," CRIED ANOTHER, "AND I'LL FIGHT ANYONE TO GET HIM."

"I SHALL BE HUSBAND TO NONE OF YOU," TARZAN DECLARED FIRMLY.

MEANWHILE, FROM HER PRISON HUT, LINDA WATCHED IN FEARFUL BEWILDERMENT. TARZAN'S EYES CAUGHT HERS.

AN AMAZON SAW THEIR INTERCHANGE OF GLANCES. HER FACE LIGHTED WITH UNDERSTANDING AS SHE SHOUTED: "THERE! HE SCORNS US BECAUSE HE LOVES THE CAPTIVE. SHE MUST DIE!"

NEXT WEEK: TARZAN'S FALL

HOGARTH—

Tarzan
by EDGAR RICE BURROUGHS

436-7-16-39

TARZAN'S FALL

THE JEALOUS HATRED OF THE AMAZONS WAS TURNED ON LINDA, FOR THEY BELIEVED TARZAN LOVED HER.

"KILL HER! HURL HER TO THE GROUND!" THEY CRIED, RACING TO HER PRISON HUT.

AS THEY DRAGGED HER OUT, TARZAN KNEW HE MUST ACT AT ONCE. BUT WHAT COULD HE DO?

STEPPING FORWARD AS IF TO PROTEST, HE TRIPPED AT THE EDGE OF THE PLATFORM.

THE HORRIFIED AMAZONS SAW HIS BODY HURTLING DOWN UNTIL IT VANISHED IN THE FOLIAGE BELOW.

Copt. 1939, Edgar Rice Burroughs Inc—Tm Reg. U.S. Pat. Off. Produced by Famous Books and Plays. Distributed by UNITED FEATURE SYNDICATE, Inc.

LINDA SCREAMED. THE MAN SHE LOVED, HER DEFENDER HAD FALLEN PERHAPS TO HIS DEATH.

MOST OF THE WARRIOR WOMEN SWARMED DOWN ANXIOUSLY TO LEARN HIS FATE.

BUT TARZAN'S FALL HAD BEEN A CLEVER TRICK. HE CLUTCHED A BRANCH AND HALTED HIS PLUNGE.

THEN, SCREENED BY LEAFY BRANCHES, HE MOUNTED TO LINDA'S BALCONY, WHERE A FEW UNWARY GUARDS REMAINED.

AS TARZAN SEIZED THE GIRL AND FLED, THE AMAZONS WHEELED, THUNDERSTRUCK.

BUT THEIR SURPRISE TURNED QUICKLY TO FURY. NO MAN COULD MAKE FOOLS OF THEM!

SO, WITH SHRILL CRIES OF RAGE, THEY FLUNG THEMSELVES FORWARD IN FRANTIC PURSUIT.

HOGARTH—

NEXT WEEK:- A SAD DUTY-

437-7-23-39

Tarzan

by Edgar Rice Burroughs

Edgar Rice Burroughs, Inc.—Tm. Reg. U. S. Pat.
Off. Produced in Famous Books and Plays. Distributed by
UNITED FEATURE SYNDICATE, Inc.

A SAD DUTY

LIKE DARTING BIRDS OF PREY THE AMAZONS WERE OVERHAULING THE HANDICAPPED APE-MAN.

HE SWERVED SWIFTLY AND DROPPED DOWN TO A TREELESS PLAIN. AS HE HAD FORESEEN---

---THE WARRIOR WOMEN ABANDONED THE CHASE, FEARING THE LIONS THAT MIGHT LIE HIDDEN IN THE GRASS.

SO TARZAN BORE LINDA SAFELY TO THEIR JUNGLE RETREAT. HERE HE LEFT HER AND WENT OUT TO HUNT.

WHILE TARZAN WAS GONE, LINDA CAUGHT SIGHT OF A SAFARI FILING ALONG A JUNGLE TRAIL.

SHE UTTERED A HAPPY CRY, FOR THE LEADER WAS HER FATHER, WHO HAD COME TO SEARCH FOR HER.

"NOW WE'RE GOING HOME," DR. FARR REJOICED. LINDA PROTESTED. SHE WISHED TO REMAIN WITH HER "WILD MAN."

DR. FARR, ENFEEBLED BY ILLNESS, COLLAPSED AT HER WORDS. LINDA FEARED HE WOULD DIE IF SHE PERSISTED.

DUTIFULLY, SADLY, SHE STARTED HOMEWARD AT ONCE. SHE DARED NOT TRUST HERSELF TO SEE HER "TREE-MAN" AGAIN.

TOWARD SUNSET, TARZAN RETURNED AND FOUND LINDA GONE.

HE READ THE SPOOR OF THE SAFARI AND BELIEVED SHE HAD BEEN TAKEN PRISONER.

HOGARTH

SPEEDILY HE SET OUT TO FOLLOW THE TRAIL.
NEXT WEEK: **NET OF DESTINY**

Tarzan

by EDGAR RICE BURROUGHS

NET OF DESTINY

UNERRINGLY TARZAN TRAILED THE SAFARI, AND FOUND LINDA SAFE WITH HER FATHER, HOMEWARD BOUND.

IT WAS BETTER SO, HE THOUGHT. SHE HAD BEEN A PLEASING COMPANION, BUT SHE WAS UNSUITED FOR JUNGLE HARDSHIPS.

AS THE SAFARI JOURNEYED FROM THE WILDERNESS, TARZAN UNSEEN, UNHEARD, KEPT WATCH OVER ITS SAFETY.

AT LAST HE TURNED HOMEWARD, EXPECTING A PERIOD OF PEACEFUL LEISURE, BUT----

----EXTRAORDINARY EVENTS FAR TO THE SOUTH WERE WEAVING A NET OF DESTINY TO ENSNARE THE MIGHTY TARZAN. IN BULEGALAND, A WANDERING PROSPECTOR WAS WINNING THE FAVOR OF THE BLACKS WITH LAVISH PRESENTS.

AS HE DUG ONE DAY NEAR A STREAM, HIS EYES FLASHED WITH GREEDY EXCITEMENT, "DIAMONDS!"

BUT THE STONES WERE SMALL AND FEW. BETTER DEPOSITS, HE BELIEVED, EXISTED BEYOND THE MOUNTAINS.

"COME!" WE SHALL GO THERE!" HE TOLD HIS BULEGA HELPERS. THE FRIGHTENED BLACKS SHOOK THEIR HEADS.

"THAT LAND BELONG MYNHEER VAN BOEREN," SAID ONE."IF WE GO THERE, HIM CALL TARZAN. TARZAN KILL."

THE PROSPECTOR GATHERED THAT THIS MYSTERIOUS TARZAN WAS GUARDIAN OF THE LANDS OF BOTH BLACKS AND WHITES.

HOGARTH—

BUT KLAAS VANGER WAS UNDAUNTED. HIS SINISTER TRICKERY HAD ALWAYS TRIUMPHED OVER HIS FOES!
NEXT WEEK— VILLAINY —

Tarzan

by EDGAR RICE BURROUGHS

439-8-6-39

VILLAINY

THE VILLAINOUS PROSPECTOR YEARNED FOR JAN VAN BOEREN'S FARM, WHICH HE BELIEVED ABOUNDED IN DIAMONDS.

SOMEHOW HE MUST INCITE THE BULEGAS TO HELP HIM SEIZE THE SETTLER'S LANDS. SO HE LIED TO THE CHIEF: "I'VE LEARNED THE WHITES WANT MORE TERRITORY. THEY PLAN TO ATTACK YOU!"

KUNDILA WAS THUNDERSTRUCK. "BUT TARZAN MADE PEACE BETWEEN US, AND GUARANTEED OUR FRONTIER."

"TARZAN IS NOT HERE," VANGER LAUGHED, "SO YOUR ONLY DEFENSE IS TO DRIVE THE WHITES AWAY."

THE WILD YOUNG WARRIORS THIRSTED FOR BLOOD. THEY DANCED AND SHOUTED AND BEAT THE DRUMS OF WAR.

BUT KUNDILA WANTED PEACE, AND HE DISPATCHED A SECRET MESSENGER TO FIND TARZAN.

OUT ON THE GREAT VELDT, THE WAR-LIKE SOUNDS CAME TO THE EARS OF JAN VAN BOEREN, PATRIARCH OF THE SETTLERS.

MATEA, HIS ELDEST DAUGHTER, TREMBLED. SHE KNEW THE UNSPEAKABLE HORRORS OF SAVAGE WARFARE.

"IF ONLY TARZAN WERE HERE," SHE SIGHED. "HE WILL BE," SAID DIRIK, HER BROTHER, "AS SOON AS I CAN FIND HIM."

SO, TWO CONFLICTING COURIERS SPED NORTH, EACH TO ENLIST THE APE-MAN'S AID FOR HIS OWN CAUSE.

AND TARZAN, CRUISING HOMEWARD, WAS FATED TO BE DELUGED BY THE GATHERING STORM OF VIOLENCE!
NEXT WEEK: BETWEEN TWO FIRES

Tarzan
by Edgar Rice Burroughs

BETWEEN TWO FIRES

AS TARZAN NEARED HIS JUNGLE HOME, THE BREATHLESS BULEGA MESSENGER FOUND HIM. "O, BIG BWANA, COME QUICK! THE WHITE SETTLERS THREATEN TO DRIVE US FROM OUR LANDS."

"I'LL HELP YOU," TARZAN AGREED, "FOR JAN VAN BOEREN PROMISED THAT HIS PEOPLE WOULD NOT DISTURB YOU."

AS HE SPOKE, A WHITE MAN APPEARED OUT OF THE WILDERNESS AND SPRANG WITH COLD FURY ON THE BLACK.

IN A MOMENT THEY WERE FIGHTING DESPERATELY, BUT TARZAN'S MIGHTY HANDS WRENCHED THEM APART.

"DIRIK VAN BOEREN! WHAT'S THE MEANING OF THIS?" THE JUNGLE LORD DEMANDED STERNLY.

BOTH COURIERS SPOKE, EACH ACCUSING THE OTHERS' PEOPLE OF PLANS FOR BLOODY AGGRESSION.

TARZAN SENSED SOME MYSTERIOUS INTRIGUE. "I GO-----SWIFTLY, ALONE. YOU TWO WILL FOLLOW."

TO ASSURE THE COURIERS' SAFE RETURN, HE CLEVERLY APPOINTED EACH THE GUARDIAN OF THE OTHER.

---MEANWHILE, KLAAS VANGER CONTINUED TO EXCITE THE BLOOD LUST OF THE YOUNG WARRIORS AGAINST THE WHITES.

FROM A CONFIDANT OF THE CHIEF, WHOM HE MADE DRUNK, HE LEARNED THAT TARZAN WAS EXPECTED SOON.

VANGER RESOLVED TO GOAD THE BULEGAS TO ATTACK AT ONCE, AND HE HIT UPON A TRICK TO DO IT!

NEXT WEEK: TRICKERY

HOGARTH

Tarzan

by EDGAR RICE BURROUGHS

TRICKERY

KUNDILA PRAYED TO HIS LITTLE IDOL THAT TARZAN WOULD COME SOON TO RESTRAIN HIS WILD YOUNG WARRIORS.

BUT VANGER WAS INFLAMING THEM TO DRIVE AWAY THE SETTLERS WHOSE LAND HE COVETED FOR HIS DIAMOND SEARCH.

AND HE CONCEIVED A VILE SCHEME TO PROVOKE THE ATTACK AT ONCE.

PRETENDING THAT HE HAD LEFT SOME TOOLS NEAR THE BORDER, HE DISPATCHED A BULEGA TO FETCH THEM.

SECRETLY VANGER FOLLOWED, AND SHOT THE POOR FELLOW FROM AMBUSH.

TO THE BULEGAS HE REPORTED THAT THE WHITES HAD VIOLATED THE FRONTIER AND SLAIN THEIR COMRADE.

THE SEETHING VOLCANO OF WRATH EXPLODED. THE FURIOUS WARRIORS SWEPT DOWN TO THE VELDT.

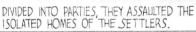

DIVIDED INTO PARTIES, THEY ASSAULTED THE ISOLATED HOMES OF THE SETTLERS.

TARZAN, NEARING HIS GOAL, HEARD THE GHASTLY TUMULT OF WAR.

"YOU HAVE BROKEN YOUR PROMISE OF PEACE," HE CRIED, "AND I WILL HELP THOSE YOU FIGHT!"

HOGARTH

SEEING JAN VAN BOEREN'S HOME UNDER ATTACK, HE DASHED INTO THE MIDST OF THE RAIDERS.

NEXT WEEK: GROOT CARLUS

"TARZAN IS AGAINST US," SHOUTED THE WARRIORS. "BULLALLA! BULLALLA! KILL! KILL!"

Tarzan

by Edgar Rice Burroughs

GROOT CARLUS

442-8-27-39

THE FOREMOST JABBED HIS SPEAR. THE APE-MAN WRENCHED IT AWAY AND TURNED IT AGAINST HIS ASSAILANT

KNOWING TARZAN'S FIGHTING POWER, THE SURROUNDING WARRIORS SOUGHT TO FINISH HIM QUICKLY.

DODGING, FEINTING, PLUNGING, THRUSTING, TARZAN FOUGHT VALIANTLY AGAINST OVERWHELMING ODDS.

BUT WITH SO MANY SPEARS AGAINST HIM, HE MUST SURELY FALL VICTIM TO ONE OF THEM.

THROUGH A LOOP HOLE, JAN VAN BOEREN SAW TARZAN'S PLIGHT. "I MUST GO OUT TO HELP HIM," HE SAID.

"NO, I WILL GO," THE SLOW DEEP VOICE CAME FROM AN UGLY HULK OF A MAN STANDING BESIDE HIM.

THIS WAS A FARM WORKER, CARLUS DE JONG, CALLED GROOT CARLUS BECAUSE OF HIS GREAT SIZE.

"I WILL GO," GROOT CARLUS REPEATED. "YOU, JAN, HAVE A FAMILY. I HAVE NO ONE---- ---WHO CARES FOR ME."

Copr. 1939, Edgar Rice Burroughs, Inc.—Tm. Reg. U. S. Pat. Off. Reproducing for Feature's Writers and Fans. Distributed by UNITED FEATURE SYNDICATE, Inc.

HIS BIG WISTFUL EYES SHIFTED FOR A MOMENT TO MATEA, THEN TURNED SHYLY AWAY.

CARLUS DREW VAN BOEREN FROM THE DOOR AND SAID: "BE READY TO CLOSE IT QUICKLY WHEN I GO."

THE GIANT LEAPED OUT AND RAN TOWARD TARZAN; BUT BEFORE THE DOOR COULD BE CLOSED------

HOGARTH—

--HALF A DOZEN SAVAGES THRUST THEMSELVES THROUGH!
NEXT WEEK: **THE MISSING GIRL**

132   Tarzan and the Boers, Part II

Tarzan

by EDGAR RICE BURROUGHS

443-9-3-39

HURLING THEMSELVES AGAINST THE DOOR, SEVERAL OF THE SAVAGES PENETRATED THE VAN BOEREN HOUSEHOLD.

MEANWHILE IN GIANT STRIDES, GROOT CARLUS HURRIED TO TARZAN'S SIDE.

THERE HE FOUGHT SLOWLY, AWKWARDLY, BUT WITH CRUSHING EFFECT— A MASSIVE ENGINE OF DESTRUCTION.

THE APE-MAN DELIGHTED IN HIS STRANGE NEW ALLY, AND TOGETHER THEY ACCOUNTED FOR MANY A SAVAGE.

PRESENTLY, SHOUTS FROM THE HOUSE CLAIMED TARZAN'S ATTENTION. "THEY NEED US THERE!" HE SAID.

Copt. 1939. Edgar Rice Burroughs, Inc.—Tm. Reg. U. S. Pat. Off. Produced by Famous Books and Plays. Distributed by UNITED FEATURE SYNDICATE, Inc.

IN THE HOUSE THE BATTLE WAS RAGING FROM ROOM TO ROOM IN WILD CONFUSION.

THE STRATEGY OF THE SAVAGES WAS TO SEPARATE THE DEFENDERS.

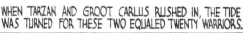

WHEN TARZAN AND GROOT CARLUS RUSHED IN, THE TIDE WAS TURNED FOR THESE TWO EQUALED TWENTY WARRIORS.

UNDER THEIR MIGHTY BLOWS, THE REMNANT OF THE WARRIORS FLED.

THEN TARZAN HURRIED AWAY TO RELIEVE SOME OTHER BESIEGED HOMESTEAD.

HOGARTH—

SOON AFTER HE LEFT, VROUW VAN BOEREN GLANCED ABOUT ANXIOUSLY THEN CALLED THROUGH THE HOUSE, "MATEA—MATEA."

WHEN NO ANSWER CAME, HER MOTHERLY EYES FILLED WITH TEARS. MATEA WAS GONE!
NEXT WEEK: *A DANGEROUS TRAIL*

Tarzan
by Edgar Rice Burroughs
A Dangerous Trail

GONE! MATEA GONE! THE SHOCK FELL LIKE A PALL ON THE VAN BOEREN HOUSEHOLD.

OLD JAN SHOOK HIS HEAD. "WE'D ONLY LOSE OUR LIVES, WITHOUT HELPING HER. WAIT UNTIL TARZAN RETURNS."

"THE SAVAGES TOOK HER! WE MUST GO TO SAVE HER!" GROOT CARLUS URGED.

BUT TARZAN WAS FAR AWAY, FIGHTING THE SAVAGE INVADERS. HE MIGHT BE LONG DELAYED.

SO CARLUS DID NOT WAIT. HE SLIPPED OUT TO THE DARK VELDT, GRIMLY BOUND FOR BULEGALAND.

THE GREAT-HEARTED GIANT DID NOT STOP TO MEASURE HIS PERIL. HE LOVED MATEA. HE MUST GO TO HER.

MEANWHILE, IN THE BULEGA VILLAGE, KLAAS VANGER AWAITED REPORTS OF THE RAID HE HAD PROVOKED.

FINALLY A WARRIOR RETURNED WITH NEWS THAT TARZAN HAD DRIVEN THE ATTACKERS FROM THE VAN BOEREN FARM.

"ALWAYS THAT CONFOUNDED TARZAN!" VANGER MUTTERED. "I MUST FIND A WAY TO DESTROY HIM."

"BUT WE TOOK A CAPTIVE," THE WARRIOR GRINNED, POINTING TO A GIRL BESIDE THE CAMPFIRE.

"WHO IS SHE?" "MYNHEER VAN BOEREN'S DAUGHTER," THE SAVAGE ANSWERED.

VANGER SMILED. ALREADY HE WAS CONTRIVING TO USE THIS GIRL IN HIS EVIL SCHEME!
NEXT WEEK: **VISITOR IN THE NIGHT**

Tarzan

by Edgar Rice Burroughs

445-9-17-39

VISITOR IN THE NIGHT

INFORMED OF MATEA'S CAPTURE, TARZAN SPED TOWARD THE DISTANT STRONGHOLD OF THE SAVAGES.

BUT GROOT CARLUS ALREADY WAS ENTERING THE VILLAGE, REJOICING WHEN HE SAW THAT MATEA WAS STILL ALIVE. SIMPLE CARLUS HAD NO CLEVER PLAN TO OUTWIT THE SAVAGES. HE MERELY STALKED FORWARD, MUSKET READY.

"I'VE COME FOR THE GIRL," HE SAID, ADVANCING SLOWLY. "I'LL KILL THE FIRST MAN THAT MOVES."

HIS BOLD VENTURE MIGHT HAVE SUCCEEDED HAD HE NOT STUMBLED AWK-WARDLY, SPRAWLING TO THE GROUND.

AS HIS POUNCING FOES DRAGGED HIM TO HIS FEET, HE TURNED HIS GREAT EYES TO MATEA IN MEEK APOLOGY.

"I-I HAD HOPED TO SAVE YOU," HE STAMMERED. "I'M SORRY." WITH A BRAVE SMILE MATEA CONCEALED HER ANGER AT HIS CLUMSY BUNGLING.

HIDDEN IN HIS HUT, KLAAS VANGER WITNESSED THE CAPTURE OF GROOT CARLUS.

"TOMORROW, YOU MAY KILL THE FOOL!" HE TOLD HIS SAVAGE HENCHMAN. "AS FOR THE GIRL----"

VANGER LEANED CLOSE AND WHISPERED HIS INSTRUCTIONS. AN HOUR LATER, WHEN THE CAMP SLEPT--

---MATEA WAS CONSCIOUS OF A FIGURE SLINKING UP BESIDE HER THROUGH THE DARKNESS OF HER PRISON HUT!

NEXT WEEK: **CHALLENGE ACCEPTED**

Tarzan

by EDGAR RICE BURROUGHS

446-9-24-39

CHALLENGE ACCEPTED

"WHO ARE YOU?" MATEA DEMANDED. "A FRIEND---TO SAVE YOU," THE CREEPING FIGURE ANSWERED.

TRUSTFULLY MATEA FOLLOWED, AND KLAAS VANGER LED HER PAST THE SENTRY WHO WAS ONLY FEIGNING SLEEP. VANGER HAD ARRANGED THE "FAKE RESCUE"-- BECAUSE HIS NEW SCHEME DEPENDED ON WINNING MATEA'S FAVOR.

AS THEY TRAVELED TOWARD THE VAN BOEREN HOME, TARZAN WAS SPEEDING BY ANOTHER ROUTE TO THE BULEGA VILLAGE.

ARRIVING AT DAWN, HE HEARD A GREAT COMMOTION. INTO THE TREES HE LEAPED AND HASTENED TOWARD IT.

UNITED FEATURE SYNDICATE Inc

HE SAW A BAND OF WARRIORS PREPARING TO EXECUTE GROOT CARLUS, HIS FAITHFUL FRIEND.

THE VENGEFUL WARRIORS TIED THE GIANT TO A TREE, TO PIERCE HIM WITH SPEARS.

GROOT CARLUS MADE NO COMPLAINT. HE ASKED NO MERCY. HE HAD GAMBLED HIS LIFE FOR MATEA-AND LOST.

"I WISH IT WERE TARZAN TIED TO A TREE," SCOWLED A WARRIOR WHO HAD FELT THE APE-MAN'S BLOWS.

"I WOULD NOT WISH TARZAN TIED. I'D FIGHT HIM HAND TO HAND," THEIR LEADER BOASTED. HE STRUTTED BEFORE HIS COMRADES, INVITING ADMIRATION OF HIS LONG-DISTANCE CHALLENGE.

HOGARTH—

THEN, SUDDENLY, A FIGURE DROPPED DOWN FROM THE TREES. THE FIGURE SPOKE "TARZAN IS HERE!"
NEXT WEEK: MYSTERY

Tarzan

by Edgar Rice Burroughs

447-10-1-39

MYSTERY

AS GAWA BOASTED WHAT HE WOULD DO TO TARZAN IN SINGLE COMBAT, THE APE-MAN DROPPED DOWN AMONG THE ASTONISHED WARRIORS. "CHOOSE YOUR WEAPON," THE JUNGLE LORD SAID CALMLY. "TARZAN NEEDS NONE!"

GAWA WAS AWED BY TARZAN'S BOLDNESS, BUT HE DARED NOT REVEAL HIS FEAR TO HIS COMRADES.

THE YOUNG WARRIOR LURCHED FORWARD WITH HIS SPEAR. TARZAN STEPPED LAUGHINGLY ASIDE.

AGAIN AND AGAIN THE BULEGA RUSHED. EACH TIME THE APE-MAN DODGED, UNTIL GAWA WAS COMPLETELY UNNERVED.

THEN TARZAN DASHED IN, SEIZED HIM, AND FLUNG HIM TO THE GROUND. GAWA ROSE WEAKLY BOWING IN DEFEAT.

THE JUNGLE LORD HURRIED TO GROOT CARLUS, AND CUT THE ROPES THAT BOUND HIM.

"NOW WHERE IS THE GIRL YOU CAPTURED?" TARZAN DEMANDED OF THE WARRIORS.

"ESCAPED. I WAS ON GUARD. I FELL ASLEEP," VANGER'S ACCOMPLICE LIED.

HOGARTH—

"BULEGA GUARDS DO NOT FALL ASLEEP," TARZAN FROWNED. HE SUSPECTED SOME MYSTERY HERE.

AND HE MIGHT HAVE FORCED THE FELLOW TO REVEAL VANGER'S PART IN THE AFFAIR, BUT CARLUS INTERRUPTED.

"WE HAVE NO TIME FOR QUESTIONS. THIS COUNTRY IS FULL OF FIERCE BEASTS. WE MUST FIND MATEA AT ONCE!"

NEXT WEEK: THE VILLAIN'S CHANCE

Tarzan

by Edgar Rice Burroughs

THE VILLAIN'S CHANCE

498-10-8-39

AS HE PICKED UP MATEA'S TRAIL, TARZAN SAW THAT A MAN'S FOOTPRINTS WERE MINGLED WITH HERS.

AN HOUR LATER, HE AND GROOT CARLIJS OVERTOOK THE PAIR. CARLIJS WAS OVERJOYED; TARZAN WAS PUZZLED.

THE APE-MAN GAZED SEARCHINGLY AT THE STRANGER. "WHO ARE YOU?" HE DEMANDED.

"THIS IS MYNHEER VANGER," MATEA ANSWERED PROUDLY. "HE SAVED ME FROM THE SAVAGES."

"YES," VANGER BOASTED, "I WAS TRAVELING NEARBY WHEN I SAW HER BROUGHT IN A CAPTIVE."

"IS IT YOUR CUSTOM TO TRAVEL THE JUNGLE AT NIGHT?" TARZAN ASKED COLDLY. THE MAN BEGAN TO STUTTER.

MATEA BROKE IN ANGRILY. "WHY MUST A HERO BE CROSS-EXAMINED LIKE A CRIMINAL?"

TARZAN DID NOT ANSWER, FOR HIS KEEN NOSTRILS HAD CAUGHT THE SCENT OF SUDDEN DANGER.

AT THE NEXT MOMENT A LEOPARD BROKE FROM THE UNDERBRUSH, CHARGING STRAIGHT AT THE LITTLE GROUP.

HOGARTH—

"RUN!" TARZAN CALLED TO THE OTHERS AS HE DASHED FORWARD TO MEET THE CHARGE. BUT VANGER STOOD HIS GROUND. HERE WAS HIS CHANCE TO KILL HIS FOE, WHILE SEEMING TO AIM AT THE LEOPARD.

THE BEAST SPRANG AT TARZAN. VANGER FIRED---AT TARZAN!
NEXT WEEK: **BEASTS OF THE MOUNTAIN**

Tarzan
by Edgar Rice Burroughs

449-10-15-39

BEASTS OF THE MOUNTAIN

BUT AT THAT INSTANT TARZAN WAS DODGING THE TALONS OF THE PLUNGING BEAST.

WHILE PRETENDING TO AIM AT THE CHARGING LEOPARD, KLAAS VANGER FIRED AT TARZAN.

THE BULLET CRASHED INTO THE LEOPARD'S SKULL. IT FELL DEAD.

MATEA SQUIRMED FROM THE ARMS OF GROOT CARLUS AND RAN EXCITEDLY TO VANGER.

"OH, YOU ARE SO BRAVE," SHE CRIED, "YOU STOOD YOUR GROUND AND SAVED TARZAN'S LIFE!"

TARZAN COULD HAVE KILLED THE BEAST HIMSELF, BUT HE MADE NO COMMENT. NOR DID HE SUSPECT VANGER'S EVIL DESIGNS.

"WITH SUCH AN EXPERT MARKSMAN YOU'LL BE SAFE," HE SAID. "I'LL RETURN ACROSS THE MOUNTAINS."

"NO, DON'T!" GROOT CARLUS WARNED. "TERRIBLE BABOONS LIVE THERE. THEY KILL MEN---TEAR THEM TO PIECES!"

BUT THE WARNING ONLY EXCITED TARZAN'S CURIOSITY. HE SET OUT TOWARD THE DESOLATE MOUNTAINS.

HE WENT WARILY, FOR NO BREEZE STIRRED TO BRING HIM THE SCENT OF LURKING DANGERS.

SUDDENLY A BAND OF BABOONS ROSE UP FROM BEHIND THE BOULDERS, SNARLING THEIR HOSTILITY!

NEXT WEEK: DOUBLE DANGER

HOGARTH—

Tarzan

by EDGAR RICE BURROUGHS

DOUBLE DANGER

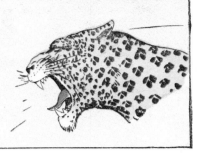

EVEN THE MIGHTY TARZAN DARED NOT ADVANCE IN THE FACE OF THE FEROCIOUS BABOONS.

YET, HE DARED NOT RETREAT, FOR IN THE JUNGLE HE MUST REMAIN SUPREME MASTER OF MEN AND BEASTS. "I TARZAN-FRIEND," HE SAID. THE BEASTS WERE PUZZLED BY THE MAN WHO SPOKE THEIR LANGUAGE.

BUT THE BABOON KING ADVANCED ANGRILY. "ALL MAN-THINGS ENEMIES," HE SNARLED. "BO-DEK'S BULLS KILL!"

KNOWING HE COULD NOT HOPE TO BEST THEM ALL, TARZAN CUNNINGLY PLANNED TO LIMIT THE COMBAT.

"BO-DEK FEARS TO FIGHT TARZAN ALONE," HE GROWLED. THE BABOON KING TOOK THIS AS A PERSONAL INSULT.

"BO-DEK KILL!" HE BARKED, AND CROUCHED FOR THE SPRING THAT WOULD DRIVE HIS FANGS INTO TARZAN'S THROAT.

THEN, FROM A NEARBY RAVINE CAME A PANICKY SCREAM, FOLLOWED BY THE HUNGRY GROWL OF A LEOPARD.

FORGETTING TARZAN, BO-DEK RACED TO DEFEND HIS MATE AND BALU FROM THE SAVAGE FELINE

THE APE-MAN DARTED PAST, LEAPED DOWN UPON THE LEOPARD'S BACK, AND DROVE HIS KNIFE INTO ITS SIDE.

HOGARTH—

THE BEAST ROARED, TOTTERED, AND FELL CRAZILY SO THAT TARZAN WAS PINNED BENEATH THE CARCASS.

AND BEFORE HE COULD FREE HIMSELF, THE DEAD LEOPARD'S MATE CHARGED DOWN TO TAKE REVENGE
NEXT WEEK: SEALED IN BLOOD!

Tarzan

by EDGAR RICE BURROUGHS

451-10-29-39

SEALED IN BLOOD

AS TARZAN WAS STRUGGLING FREE OF HIS VICTIM'S CARCASS, THE SHE-LEOPARD SPRANG AT HIM. AT THE SAME MOMENT, A FLYING BULK FLASHED PAST HIM. IT WAS BO-DEK.

THE BABOON'S FANGS SANK INTO THE LEOPARD'S THROAT AND RIPPED ITS JUGULAR VEIN.

BEFORE TARZAN COULD JOIN THE FRAY, THE BEAST FELL DEAD. BO-DEK AND TARZAN STARED ADMIRINGLY AT EACH OTHER.

THEY HAD RISKED THEIR LIVES TOGETHER. THEIR FRIENDSHIP WAS SEALED IN THE BLOOD OF THE CONQUERED FOE.

NOW BO-DEK LED HIS TRIBE TO THEIR RAVINE REFUGE. TARZAN RETURNED TO THE VAN BOEREN'S, WHERE----

-HE FOUND KLAAS VANGER ESTABLISHED IN THE BOSOM OF THE FAMILY BECAUSE OF HIS "HEROIC RESCUE" OF MATEA.

"I'VE MADE PEACE WITH THE SAVAGES," TARZAN REPORTED. "BUT I'LL STAY UNTIL I DISCOVER WHO STIRRED THEM UP."

THE GUILTY VANGER TREMBLED INWARDLY. HE MUST FIND A WAY TO DESTROY THIS MEDDLING FELLOW!

NEXT DAY, VANGER SET OUT FOR A HUNT. GROOT CARLUS WARNED HIM, POINTING TO A DISTANT RAVINE.

"KEEP CLEAR OF DUIVELSKLOOF! FIERCE BABOONS LIVE THERE. WE LEAVE THEM ALONE--- THEY LEAVE US ALONE!"

NEXT WEEK: VANGER'S LUCK

BUT ONCE OUT OF SIGHT, VANGER TURNED TOWARD THE DARK, MYSTERIOUS RAVINE! -HOGARTH—

Tarzan

by Edgar Rice Burroughs

452-11-5-39

VANGER'S LUCK

KLAAS VANGER ENTERED THE STRANGE VALLEY, HIS EYES GLUED ON THE PEBBLY BED OF A STREAM.

SUDDENLY HE DROPPED TO HIS KNEE AND CLAWED AT THE GRAVEL. "BLINK KLIPPERS---BRIGHT STONES!" HE CRIED.

HE SCRATCHED UNTIL HIS FINGERS BLED, AND SOON HE HAD FILLED HIS MONEY BELT WITH ROUGH DIAMONDS.

HE HUNG THE BELT ON A BUSH AND WANDERED UPSTREAM EXPLORING THE EXTENT OF HIS FABULOUS DISCOVERY.

SO INTENT WAS HE THAT HE DID NOT NOTICE THE BABOONS WATCHING HIM FROM THE ROCKY SLOPE.

BO-DEK WAS FURIOUS AT THIS INVASION OF THEIR REFUGE, AND HE RESOLVED TO TAKE BLOOD-VENGEANCE.

"KILL!" HE COMMANDED; AND HIS FIERCE BULLS CREPT DOWN TO SPRING UPON THE UNWELCOME STRANGER.

VANGER SUDDENLY TURNED AND SAW THE STALKING BABOONS. HE FIRED. ONE OF THE BEASTS FELL.

NOW THAT THEIR AMBUSH HAD FAILED, THE BABOONS FEARED THE DEADLY THUNDER-STICK. THEY FLED.

TARZAN HEARD THE GUNFIRE AND KNEW THAT HIS FRIENDS, THE BABOONS, WERE IN TROUBLE.

VANGER CONTINUED TO FIRE! HE'D TEACH THESE DEVILISH BEASTS A LESSON!

HOGARTH—

NEXT WEEK: THE VILLAIN'S TRICK

TARZAN RACED DOWN, TO HALT THE SLAUGHTER, UNAWARE THAT VANGER WOULD WELCOME A CHANCE TO KILL HIM.

Tarzan

by Edgar Rice Burroughs

453-11-12-39

THE VILLAIN'S TRICK

AS VANGER FIRED, THE BABOONS FLED IN PANIC. BO-DEK, GLANCING BACK AS HE RAN, BLUNDERED INTO VANGER'S DIAMOND-STUFFED MONEY-BELT HUNG ON A BUSH.

THE BELT FELL ACROSS HIS SHOULDER LIKE A BANDOLEER. FRIGHTENED BY THE CLINGING THING, HE RAN EVEN FASTER.

VANGER WAS DISMAYED BY THE STRANGE ACCIDENT THAT GAVE THE BABOON POSSESSION OF THE DIAMONDS. HE FIRED.

THE BULLET RIPPED BO-DEK'S ARM, BUT DID NOT STOP HIM. PRESENTLY HE VANISHED AMONG THE BOULDERS.

VANGER CONTINUED FIRING AS THE BABOONS EXPOSED THEMSELVES IN THEIR MAD RACE UP THE SLOPE.

THEN TARZAN APPEARED BEHIND VANGER AND WHIRLED HIM AROUND. "WHY DO YOU KILL THE BABOONS?" HE DEMANDED.

"THEY---I MEAN, I DON'T LIKE THEM," THE PROSPECTOR SNARLED IN REPLY.

"NOR DO I LIKE YOU," TARZAN SAID. "BUT I SHALL NOT KILL YOU---UNLESS YOU GIVE ME REASON."

A MURDEROUS ANGER FLAMED IN VANGER'S HEART. HERE WAS AN OPPORTUNITY TO RID HIMSELF OF THIS INTERFERING SAVAGE.

HE WOULD TRY A TRICK TO THROW TARZAN OFF GUARD. "LOOK OUT BEHIND YOU!" HE SHOUTED IN MOCK DISMAY.

NEXT WEEK: TARZAN'S ERROR

AT THE SAME MOMENT HIS FINGERS TIGHTENED ON HIS RIFLE TO SHOOT WHEN TARZAN TURNED.

HOGARTH—

Tarzan

TARZAN'S ERROR

by EDGAR RICE BURROUGHS

454-11-19-39

WHEN VANGER YELLED, "LOOK OUT BEHIND!" TARZAN DID NOT MOVE.

THE WIND WAS AT HIS BACK AND HIS KEEN NOSTRILS BROUGHT HIM NO SCENT OF DANGER.

"TRICKSTER!" HE GROWLED. "YOU ONLY WANTED A CHANCE TO KILL ME!" AT THE SAME INSTANT HE GRASPED VANGER'S RIFLE.

WITH ONE MIGHTY BLOW TARZAN BROKE THE GUN, THEN COMMANDED, "GO! IF YOU RETURN TO THIS VALLEY, YOU DIE!"

VANGER WAS GLAD ENOUGH TO ESCAPE WITH HIS LIFE, BUT THE EXPERIENCE STRENGTHENED HIS RESOLVE TO DESTROY TARZAN.

THE APE-MAN TURNED UP THE MOUNTAIN SLOPE TO AID THE WOUNDED BABOONS.

ALREADY ON THE PLATEAU, THE REMNANT OF THE TRIBE WAS GATHERING ABOUT THE BABOON KING.

BO-DEK TUGGED AT VANGER'S DIAMOND-FILLED MONEY BELT WHICH SO ODDLY HAD FALLEN ON HIM.

IT BORE THE HATED HUMAN SCENT AND HE HASTENED TO BE RID OF IT, BUT LU-DEK, HIS MATE, STOPPED HIM.

SHE STEPPED BACK AND GAZED APPROVINGLY. OTHERS, TOO, LOOKED AT HIM WITH AWE. SO BO-DEK CAME TO REGARD THE BELT PROUDLY AS A SYMBOL OF HIS MIGHT AND MAJESTY.

NEXT WEEK: PLANS FOR MURDER

HOGARTH

THEN TARZAN ARRIVED WITH NEWS THAT THEIR FOE HAD FLED, AND WOULD NEVER RETURN. BUT TARZAN WAS WRONG!

Tarzan

by Edgar Rice Burroughs

PLANS FOR MURDER

455-11-26-39

WHEN BO-DEK BOASTED THAT HIS BANDOLEER WAS A TROPHY OF BATTLE, TARZAN GREW CURIOUS.

BUT THE BABOON-KING WAS UNABLE TO EXPLAIN, AND THE APE-MAN THOUGHT IT UNIMPORTANT.

IF TARZAN HAD KNOWN THAT THIS WAS VANGER'S DIAMOND-STUFFED BELT, HE COULD HAVE AVOIDED THE DEADLY PITFALLS AHEAD.

THE APE-MAN REMAINED SEVERAL DAYS WITH THE BABOONS, HEALING THE WOUNDED WITH JUNGLE HERBS AND BALSAMS.

WHEN HE RETURNED TO THE VAN BOERENS, THEY WERE CELEBRATING MATEA'S BETROTHAL TO KLAAS VANGER. TARZAN KNEW VANGER WAS A SCOUNDREL, AND HE WANTED TO SAVE MATEA FROM HIS SCHEMES.

HE STEPPED FORWARD THREATENINGLY. "GET OUT!" HE ORDERED. "YOU'RE NOT FIT TO MARRY THIS GIRL!"

MATEA BRISTLED. "THAT IS FOR ME TO DECIDE, MYNHEER TARZAN, AND I HAVE DECIDED."

GROOT CARLUS RESTRAINED TARZAN. "I WANTED HER," HE SIGHED, "BUT IF SHE IS HAPPY, IT IS WELL."

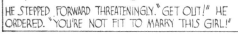

SO COMPLETELY HAD VANGER DECEIVED THE VAN BOERENS THAT ALL TOOK HIS SIDE.

NOW HE COULD PURSUE HIS PLAN TO MARRY MATEA, MURDER HER FAMILY, AND GAIN CONTROL OF THE SECRET DIAMOND RAVINE.

FIRST, HOWEVER, HE MUST GET RID OF TARZAN. THAT NIGHT HIS OPPORTUNITY CAME!

NEXT WEEK: **KRAAL OF DEATH**

HOGARTH—

Tarzan

by Edgar Rice Burroughs

456-12-3-39

KRAAL OF DEATH

A HUNGRY LEOPARD SLUNK DOWN FROM THE MOUNTAINS AND INVADED THE VAN BOEREN KRAAL. ITS SHARP FANGS SANK INTO THE BACK OF AN OX.

INSTANTLY ALL THE CATTLE WERE THROWN INTO A PANIC.

KLAAS VANGER WAS THE FIRST TO HEAR THE BELLOWING, THUNDERING TUMULT. HE GUESSED ITS MEANING.

ANXIOUS TO WIN THE FAVOR OF THE VAN BOERENS HE GRABBED A RIFLE AND DASHED TO THE KRAAL.

MEANWHILE TARZAN, SLEEPING ON THE VELDT, HEARD THE UPROAR. HE, TOO, RAN TO THE KRAAL.

FROM ATOP THE FENCE, VANGER FIRED AT THE LEOPARD---AND MISSED.

THEN TARZAN ARRIVED AND CLAMBERED UP THE FENCE. VANGER TURNED. HERE WAS HIS HATED ENEMY!

HE WAS ABOUT TO RAISE HIS GUN AND FIRE, BUT CRAFTY CAUTION STOPPED HIM.

NO! TARZAN'S DEATH MUST APPEAR ACCIDENTAL. A PLAN FLASHED IN THE VILLAIN'S MIND.

PRETENDING TO LOSE HIS BALANCE HE LURCHED AGAINST THE APE-MAN.

TARZAN TUMBLED INTO THE KRAAL WHERE, VANGER BELIEVED---

HOGARTH

HE WOULD BE TORN TO SHREDS BY THE LEOPARD OR TRAMPLED TO DEATH BY POUNDING HOOFS!
NEXT WEEK: *FATEFUL DECISION*

Tarzan

by Edgar Rice Burroughs

FATEFUL DECISION

457-12-10-39

PUSHING TARZAN INTO THE KRAAL, VANGER EXPECTED HIM TO BE KILLED BY THE LEOPARD OR THE STAMPEDING CATTLE. BUT THE APE-MAN ROSE QUICKLY.

TO AVOID THE POUNDING HOOFS HE SPRANG TO THE BACKS OF THE OXEN.

THEN HE CROSSED THE TUMULTUOUS SEA OF TERRIFIED CATTLE AND LEAPED DOWN UPON THE LEOPARD.

WHILE VANGER WATCHED PARALYZED WITH AMAZEMENT, TARZAN DISPATCHED THE SNARLING BEAST.

THEN THE APE-MAN TURNED TOWARD VANGER. THE VILLAIN RAISED HIS RIFLE.

BUT AS HE FIRED, TARZAN GRIPPED THE BARREL AND WRENCHED IT AWAY. "I'LL PUNISH YOU FOR THIS," HE GROWLED.

KLAAS VANGER JUMPED FROM THE FENCE AND RAN, WITH TARZAN IN HOT PURSUIT.

UNITED FEATURE SYNDICATE, Inc.

THEN THE VAN BOERENS STREAMED FROM THE HOUSE. VANGER RUSHED TO THEM, SCREAMING, "TARZAN'S TRYING TO KILL ME!"

"HE TRIED TO KILL ME. I ONLY WISH TO PUNISH HIM," TARZAN SAID GRIMLY.

"I BELIEVE KLAAS," MATEA FUMED. "WE ALL KNOW YOU HATE HIM, YOU BEAST--- YOU BRUTAL JUNGLE BEAST!"

THE GIRL TURNED TO HER FATHER, "YOU MUST SEND TARZAN AWAY! HE'S A MENACE TO KLAAS---AND OUR HAPPINESS." BREATHLESSLY VANGER AWAITED THE DECISION. UPON IT DEPENDED THE SUCCESS OF HIS MURDEROUS SCHEME!

NEXT WEEK: MASSACRE

HOGARTH—

"SEND TARZAN AWAY," MATEA INSISTED. "I KNOW HE MEANS TO KILL KLAAS." JAN VAN BOEREN HESITATED. KLAAS VANGER WAS HIS DAUGHTER'S FIANCE, BUT TARZAN WAS HIS STAUNCH FRIEND.

"YOU NEED NOT DECIDE," TARZAN SAID SIMPLY. THEN HE TURNED AND VANISHED IN THE NIGHT.

THE APE-MAN STRODE TOWARD THE HILLS. THERE LIFE WAS STARK AND SAVAGE BUT UNTAINTED BY HUMAN DISCORD.

VANGER WAS DELIGHTED. HE WAS RID OF TARZAN, THE ONLY OBSTACLE TO HIS DEVILISH PLANS.

NEXT DAY HE SET OUT TO HUNT. HE SKIRTED THE FORBIDDEN DUIVELSKLOOF FOR HE FEARED TARZAN.

BUT IF HE COULD FIND THE BABOONS IN THE OPEN, HE'D KILL THE ONE WHICH HAD TAKEN HIS DIAMOND-STUFFED BELT.

HE DISCOVERED THEM TREKKING ACROSS THE PLAIN. FROM AMBUSH HE OPENED FIRE.

TARZAN HEARD THE GUNFIRE, MINGLED WITH THE SCREAMS OF THE BEASTS. FROM AFAR HE SAW THE MASSACRE.

THE FRENZIED CREATURES, INSTEAD OF FLEEING, WERE CHARGING INTO THE HAIL OF BULLETS.

TARZAN HASTENED TO THE AID OF HIS FRIENDS. THEN, TO HIS DISMAY, HE SAW-----

--THREE HORSEMEN GALLOPING ACROSS THE VELDT, THEIR GUNS TRAINED ON THE HELPLESS BABOONS!
NEXT WEEK: ORPHANS OF THE VELDT

Tarzan

by EDGAR RICE BURROUGHS

ORPHAN OF THE VELDT

459-12-24-39

THE THREE HORSEMEN "THUNDERED ACROSS THE VELDT, SHOOTING AT THE BABOONS.

NOW VANGER SAW THE APE WITH HIS DIAMOND-FILLED MONEY-BELT. HE FIRED. BO-DEK FELL DEAD.

BO-DEK'S MATE HURRIED TO HIM. A BULLET PIERCED HER HEART. BO-DAN, THEIR SON, SCREAMED IN HORROR.

THEN TARZAN APPEARED AMONG THE BABOONS COMMANDING THEM TO FLEE. LITTLE BO-DAN RAN TO HIM WHIMPERING.

IN THE RETREAT, BO-DAN CLUNG TO TARZAN, HIS ONLY COMFORT IN A WORLD GROWN DARK WITH TERROR.

NOW THE HORSEMEN DASHED UP TO VANGER. ONE NOTICED THE BANDOLEER ON THE DEAD BABOON. "LOOK, DIAMONDS!" HE CRIED.

A BULLET HAD PIERCED THE BELT AND EXPOSED THE GEMS. "THEY'RE MINE," SNARLED VANGER. "I KILLED THE BEAST."

"YOU'LL SHARE THEM!" THE STRANGER GROWLED. HIS RIFLE ENFORCED HIS DEMANDS.

"THE BEAST MUST HAVE TAKEN THE BELT FROM A DEAD PROSPECTOR," ONE OF THE NEWCOMERS MUSED.

KLAAS VANGER WAS ALARMED. SUPPOSE THEY SHOULD DISCOVER THE SECRET SOURCE OF DIAMONDS. "THE BABOONS CAME FROM THAT WAY!" HE LIED, POINTING IN THE WRONG DIRECTION. THE HORSEMEN GALLOPED AWAY.

Copr. 1939 Edgar Rice Burroughs Inc.—Tm. Reg. U.S. Pat. Produced in Frames, Books and Story. Distributed by UNITED FEATURE SYNDICATE, Inc.

NEXT WEEK: -FIRE TRAP-

HOGARTH—

HE MUST CARRY OUT HIS MURDEROUS SCHEME TO GAIN CONTROL OF THE VAN BOEREN LANDS—PERHAPS TONIGHT!

Tarzan

by EDGAR RICE BURROUGHS

460-12-31-39

FIRE TRAP

WHILE TARZAN LED THE SURVIVORS OF THE BABOON TRIBE TO THEIR REFUGE---

---- KLAAS VANGER RETURNED TO THE VAN BOEREN HOME TO CARRY OUT HIS MONSTROUS PLAN.

THAT NIGHT, WHEN THE HOUSEHOLD SLEPT, HE CREPT OUT TO THE WOODPILE AND GATHERED DRY FAGGOTS.

THESE HE PLACED AT STRATEGIC POINTS IN THE HALLWAY.

THEN HE SNEAKED ALONG THE HALL, OPENING DOORS, EXTRACTING KEYS, AND LOCKING THEM FROM THE OUTSIDE.

THESE KEYS HE SLIPPED INTO A TROUSERS POCKET OF THE SNORING GROOT CARLUS.

RETURNING TO THE HALLWAY, HE LIGHTED THE FAGGOTS. FLAMES FLARED HUNGRILY.

KLAAS VANGER DASHED TO MATEA'S ROOM. "FIRE! FIRE!" HE CRIED. "I'LL SAVE YOU!"

HE SWEPT THE TERRIFIED GIRL INTO HIS ARMS AND FLED FROM THE BURNING HOUSE.

WITHIN, JAN VAN BOEREN WAS AWAKENED BY THE SCENT OF SMOKE, THE OMINOUS CRACKLE OF FLAMES.

CALLING TO HIS WIFE HE RAN TO THE DOOR. IT WAS LOCKED FROM THE OUTSIDE.

"WE'RE TRAPPED," OLD JAN SAID CALMLY. "THIS IS THE END, MY ANNA!"
NEXT WEEK:
VANGER'S PLOT

HOGARTH—

Tarzan
by Edgar Rice Burroughs

VANGER'S PLOT

TO ESCAPE THE FIRE TRAP, JAN VAN BOEREN HURLED HIMSELF AGAINST THE LOCKED DOOR. IT HELD FAST.

"LOCKED ON THE OUTSIDE, BY SOME MURDEROUS HAND," HE SAID SLOWLY. "WE'RE DOOMED."

RESIGNED AND UNAFRAID, THE OLD PATRIARCH AND HIS WIFE SANK TO THEIR KNEES AND LIFTED THEIR VOICES IN A LAST SOLEMN PRAYER.

"FORGIVE US OUR TRESPASSES, AND THOSE WHO TRESPASS AGAINST US—EVEN HIM WHO RAISED HIS HAND AGAINST US."

IN OTHER ROOMS, DIRIK AND HIS SISTER, TOO, FOUND THEMSELVES HOPELESSLY TRAPPED.

FROM AFAR, TARZAN SAW THE RISING FLAMES AND RACED ACROSS THE VELDT AT TOP SPEED.

MEANWHILE, KLAAS VANGER CARRIED MATEA FROM THE BURNING HOUSE, AND SET HER DOWN.

FROM THE WINDOWS, WHICH WERE BARRED FOR PROTECTION AGAINST SAVAGE RAIDS, CAME THE CRIES OF THE DOOMED.

"OH, KLAAS," MATEA MOANED, "WHY CAN'T THEY ESCAPE THROUGH THE DOORS? YOU MUST GO IN AND HELP THEM!"

"TOO LATE," VANGER SHRUGGED. "I'D BE BURNED TO DEATH, AND I MUST LIVE, MATEA, TO TAKE CARE OF YOU." AS THE GIRL SOBBED ON HIS SHOULDER, VANGER SMILED INWARDLY. THIS, INDEED, WAS A FINE NIGHT'S WORK.

NEXT WEEK: AN INNOCENT VICTIM

HOGARTH—

NOW, WITH ALL THE FAMILY GONE, HE'D MARRY MATEA, AND WIN CONTROL OF THE FARM AND ITS SECRET DIAMOND DEPOSIT.

Tarzan

by Edgar Rice Burroughs

AN INNOCENT VICTIM

462-1-14-40

VANGER'S PLOT SEEMED SUCCESSFUL. WITH MATEA'S FAMILY DEAD, HE'D MARRY HER AND WIN CONTROL OF THE DIAMOND LANDS.

NOW GROOT CARLUS STAGGERED FROM THE BLAZING HOUSE. THIS WAS AS VANGER PLANNED. CARLUS MIGHT BE USEFUL.

"WHERE ARE THE OTHERS?" THE GIANT PANTED. "INSIDE," MATEA SOBBED.

AT THAT MOMENT, TARZAN RACED PAST --- INTO THE FLAMES. BRAVE GROOT CARLUS FOLLOWED.

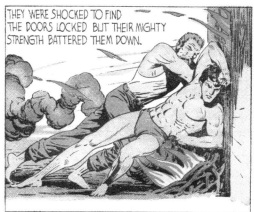

THEY WERE SHOCKED TO FIND THE DOORS LOCKED BUT THEIR MIGHTY STRENGTH BATTERED THEM DOWN.

AND TOGETHER THEY BROUGHT THE VILLAIN'S INTENDED VICTIMS TO SAFETY.

Copr. 1940 Edgar Rice Burroughs Inc. — Tm. Reg. U.S. Pat.
Off. Produced by Famous Books and Plays, distributed by
UNITED FEATURE SYNDICATE, INC.

TARZAN STRODE TOWARD VANGER. "THE DOORS WERE LOCKED," HE SAID ACCUSINGLY.

"MY DOOR WAS LOCKED, TOO," VANGER ANSWERED. "BUT IT WAS WEAK AND I BROKE IT DOWN. CARLUS DID IT."

"THAT'S NOT TRUE," GROOT CARLUS PROTESTED. "I HEARD KEYS JINGLE IN HIS POCKET," THE VILLAIN INSISTED.

"YOU LIE!" CARLUS ROARED. "SEARCH HIM," VANGER DEMANDED.

JAN VAN BOEREN PLUNGED A HAND INTO THE GIANT'S POCKET-- AND DREW OUT THREE KEYS!

CARLUS PALED. VAN BOEREN'S JAW SET STERNLY. "SO, CARLUS THE GUILT LIES ON YOUR HEAD!"
NEXT WEEK:

HOGARTH—

Tarzan

by Edgar Rice Burroughs

SCOUNDREL AT BAY

463-1-21-40

WITH ACHING HEART OLD JAN GAZED AT THE KEYS HE HAD TAKEN FROM GROOT CARLUS'S POCKET.

IT WAS UNBELIEVABLE THAT CARLUS HAD LOCKED THEM IN, TO PERISH IN THE FLAMES; YET HERE WAS PROOF. THE GIANT, THOUGH INNOCENT, WAS TOO BEWILDERED TO OFFER ANY DEFENSE.

IT WAS THE KEEN-WITTED TARZAN WHO SAW THE FLAW IN THE EVIDENCE. HE TOOK THE KEYS, THEN SPOKE:

"THERE ARE ONLY THREE—ONE FOR EACH DOOR WE BROKE DOWN. THERE'S NO KEY FOR VANGER'S DOOR. IT WAS NOT LOCKED." THE JUNGLE LORD STRODE TO VANGER, HIS FINGERS ITCHING TO THROTTLE THE SCOUNDREL.

"YOU LOCKED THOSE DOORS," HE GROWLED, "AND PUT THE KEYS IN CARLUS'S POCKET."

AS THE APE-MAN REACHED FOR HIM, THE TERRIFIED VANGER LEAPED BACK.

Copt. 1940 Edgar Rice Burroughs Inc.—Tm Reg. U S Pat Off. Produced by Famous Books and Plays, Distributed by UNITED FEATURE SYNDICATE, Inc.

THEN THE VILLAIN'S RIGHT HAND FLEW TO HIS HOLSTER. OUT FLASHED A REVOLVER.

"STAND BACK, ALL OF YOU!" HE THREATENED. "YES—I WANTED TO KILL YOU ALL——— EXCEPT MATEA!"

HOGARTH—

HIS FINGER CURLED AROUND THE TRIGGER. "NOW I'LL DO IT, AND THROW YOUR BODIES INTO THE FIRE."

VENGEANCE OF THE VELDT

HE POINTED THE GUN AT TARZAN. "YOU FIRST," HE SNARLED.

VANGER WAS IN NO HURRY TO SHOOT TARZAN. HE WAS ENJOYING THIS FINAL TRIUMPH.

MEANWHILE BO-DAN WAS STREAKING ALONG THE TRAIL OF HIS FRIEND TARZAN, WHO HAD LEFT HIM BEHIND.

WHEN THE LITTLE BABOON ARRIVED HE CAUGHT THE SCENT OF THE MAN-THING WHO HAD KILLED HIS PARENTS.

WITH A CRY OF VENGEFUL RAGE THE BEAST LEAPED FULL INTO THE FACE OF KLAAS VANGER.

AS HE SANK HIS FANGS INTO THE MAN'S CHEEK, VANGER DROPPED HIS GUN IN HIS EFFORTS TO TEAR THE BABOON AWAY.

GROOT CARLUS LEAPED AT VANGER..HE FLED. TARZAN STOOD STILL. "LET CARLUS HAVE HIS REVENGE," HE SAID.

BUT THE WILY SCOUNDREL ELUDED HIS GIANT PURSUER, AND AT LAST CARLUS RETURNED, THWARTED.

MATEA STOOD ALONE, SOBBING. HOW SHE HATED KLAAS NOW! WHAT A FOOL SHE'D BEEN TO TRUST HIS OILY TONGUE!

CARLUS CAME CLOSE, GAZING AT HER WISTFULLY, HIS GREAT LOVE FOR HER SURGING IN HIS HEART.

SMILINGLY TARZAN WHISPERED TO HIM. CARLUS NODDED, EMBRACED MATEA AWKWARDLY, AND BEGAN TO STAMMER:

"I--I'M NOT CLEVER NOR HANDSOME, BUT"--"BUT YOU'RE A REAL MAN," MATEA WHISPERED AS SHE HUGGED HIM CLOSE.

"THE OTHER ONE--VANGER-- WON'T TROUBLE US AGAIN," CARLUS DECLARED. BUT CARLUS WAS WRONG!

NEXT WEEK: VANGER STRIKES BACK

HOGARTH-

Tarzan

by Edgar Rice Burroughs

VANGER STRIKES BACK

165-2-4-40

TARZAN REMAINED AT THE VAN BOEREN FARM, HELPING TO REBUILD THE BURNED HOME.

IN THE JOY OVER THE APPROACHING MARRIAGE OF MATEA AND CARLUS, VANGER WAS FORGOTTEN.

BUT THE SCOUNDREL WAS HIDING IN THE HILLS, GROWING A BEARD AS A DISGUISE IN CASE HE WAS PURSUED.

MEANWHILE, IN THE DESOLATE COUNTRY TO THE SOUTH, SMALL DIAMOND DEPOSITS WERE DISCOVERED.

A TOWN BOOMED THERE, A TYPICAL FRONTIER TOWN--ROUGH AND READY, WILD AND LAWLESS. HERE VANGER CAME, MINGLING WITH THE MOTLEY THRONG, LAYING HIS PLANS CRAFTILY.

Copr. 1940 Edgar Rice Burroughs, Inc. — Trade Mark Reg. U. S. Pat. Off. Reproduced as Foreign Book and Mag. Reproduced by
UNITED FEATURE SYNDICATE, Inc.

HE SCORNED THE MEAGRE DIGGINGS. HE WAS AFTER THE FABULOUS DIAMOND HORDE ON THE VAN BOEREN FARM.

PATIENTLY HE GATHERED A BAND OF DESPERADOES.

WITH THEM HE SCOUTED THE VAN BOEREN LANDS, AWAITING A CHANCE TO STRIKE.

THEN ONE DAY, MATEA GALLOPED AWAY FOR A RIDE, ACCOMPANIED BY A KAFFIR SERVANT.

FROM AMBUSH VANGER SPIED THEM. "GET THE GIRL!" HE GROWLED TENSELY TO HIS HENCHMEN. SPURS DUG INTO THE HORSES. THEY LEAPED, AND RACED OUT ACROSS THE VELDT. NEXT WEEK: CAPTURED

HOGARTH—

Tarzan

by EDGAR RICE BURROUGHS

CAPTURED

466-2-11-40

ACROSS THE VELDT THE HORSEMEN GALLOPED TOWARD THE GIRL, TREACHEROUSLY ASKING HER TO WAIT. UNSUSPECTINGLY, MATEA PULLED UP HER HORSE. BUT WHEN THE MEN DREW NEAR, THEY WHIPPED OUT REVOLVERS.

SEEING HIS BELOVED MISTRESS IN DANGER, THE OLD KAFFIR TRIED TO PROTECT HER. HE WAS SHOT DOWN.

VANGER SCRIBBLED A NOTE, ATTACHED IT TO THE KAFFIR'S HORSE, AND SHOOED HIM HOMEWARD.

"YOU GO WITH US," VANGER TOLD MATEA, "AND IF YOU WANT TO LIVE YOU'LL DO AS I SAY."

WHEN THE RIDERLESS HORSE CAME GALLOPING HOME TARZAN AND CARLUS FOUND THE NOTE.

"THE GIRL WILL BE SAFE IF YOU FOLLOW THE INSTRUCTIONS I GIVE YOU LATER."

"KIDNAPED!" GROOT CARLUS GASPED. "PROBABLY VANGER'S WORK," TARZAN NODDED GRIMLY.

THEN THESE TWO RODE OUT ACROSS THE PLAIN, FOLLOWING THE BACKTRAIL OF THE RIDERLESS HORSE.

THEY PICKED UP THE TRACKS OF THE FUGITIVES, WHICH LED TO THE DIAMOND RUSH TOWN.

THERE THE HOOFPRINTS MERGED WITH A HUNDRED OTHERS. TARZAN'S QUARRY WAS LOST.

HOGARTH—

BUT THE DISGUISED VANGER SPOTTED HIS FOES, AND SIGNALED ONE OF HIS HENCHMEN! *NEXT WEEK: TRIGGER BOYLE*

Tarzan

by EDGAR RICE BURROUGHS

TRIGGER BOYLE

467-2-18-40

TARZAN AND CARLUS COULD FIND NO CLUE TO VANGER BECAUSE HE HAD DISGUISED HIS NAME AND APPEARANCE.

AS THEY DISCUSSED THEIR NEXT MOVE, LITTLE BO-DAN DREW THE ATTENTION OF THE TOWN IDLERS.

ONE OF THEM, TRIGGER BOYLE, WHISPERED TO THE CROWD, "WANT TO SEE SOMETHING FUNNY?"

HE TOSSED A PIECE OF CHEWING TOBACCO. BO-DAN CAUGHT IT EAGERLY AND SWALLOWED IT.

TURNING JUST IN TIME TO SEE THE LITTLE FELLOW'S HAND FLY TO HIS MOUTH, TARZAN WAS PUZZLED.

SOON BO-DAN PUT HIS HANDS ON HIS STOMACH. HIS EYES ROLLED PITIFULLY. HE BEGAN TO WHIMPER.

HE JUMPED UP AND DOWN, PUFFING AND BLOWING. TRIGGER LAUGHED. THE CROWD JOINED IN.

TARZAN'S FACE HARDENED. "SOMEONE GAVE THE BABOON SOMETHING TO MAKE HIM SICK, WHO WAS IT?" HE DEMANDED.

"IT WAS ME," TRIGGER SNAPPED. "WHAT'S IT TO YOU, AND WHAT'RE YOU GONNA DO ABOUT IT?"

"I INTEND TO PUNISH YOU," TARZAN SAID WITH CALM, COLD MENACE. HE STEPPED FORWARD.

THE MAN DREW HIS REVOLVER. "GET BACK! GET BACK OR I'LL SHOOT! —AND TRIGGER BOYLE NEVER MISSES."

THE FEARLESS JUNGLE LORD CONTINUED HIS STEADY STRIDE!
NEXT WEEK:
LAST WARNING

HOGARTH—

Tarzan

by EDGAR RICE BURROUGHS

LAST WARNING

468-2-25-40

"THIS IS MY LAST WARNING," THE MAN SCOWLED. "TAKE ANOTHER STEP AND I'LL PLUG YOU!" TARZAN MOVED FEARLESSLY TOWARD THE MUZZLE OF TRIGGER BOYLE'S REVOLVER.

UNNERVED BY THIS DISPLAY OF RECKLESS COURAGE, BOYLE'S GUN HAND WOBBLED.

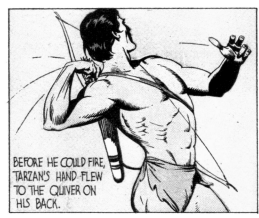

BEFORE HE COULD FIRE, TARZAN'S HAND FLEW TO THE QUIVER ON HIS BACK.

HE WHIPPED OUT AN ARROW AND FLUNG IT, WITH LIGHTNING SPEED, LIKE A DART.

THE POINT SLASHED BOYLE'S HAND. THE GUN CLATTERED TO THE GROUND. FROM THE CROWD ROSE A GASP OF AMAZEMENT.

BOYLE BACKED AWAY, DAZED AND HUMILIATED BY THE REMARKABLE FEAT OF HIS FOE.

THEN A MAN SHOULDERED HIS WAY THROUGH THE CROWD. HE WINKED SLYLY AT BOYLE, THEN DECLARED LOUDLY...

"SERVES YOU RIGHT, TRIGGER. YOU SHOULDN'T HAVE HURT THE GENTLEMAN'S LITTLE MONKEY."

THE MAN CAME UP TO TARZAN AND WHISPERED, "I HEARD YOU ASKING ABOUT A GIRL. I THINK I CAN HELP YOU!"

GROOT CARLUS SEIZED EAGERLY UPON THIS CLUE TO THE MISSING MATEA. "COME WITH ME," SAID THE STRANGER.

AS HE STROLLED AWAY, HE ROLLED HIS EYES AT TRIGGER BOYLE. THAT WAS A SECRET SIGNAL!

HOGARTH—

NEXT WEEK: *THE CLOSING TRAP*

Tarzan

by EDGAR RICE BURROUGHS

THE CLOSING TRAP

469-3-3-40

TRIGGER BOYLE CAUGHT THE SLY SIGNAL OF THE MAN WHO HAD SPOKEN TO TARZAN. HE NODDED AND HURRIED AWAY. TARZAN AND GROOT CARLUS FELL IN BEHIND THEIR MYSTERIOUS GUIDE.

THEN LITTLE BO-DAN, RECOVERING FROM HIS ILLNESS, STAGGERED DIZZILY TO HIS FEET, AND FOLLOWED.

"THE KIDNAPED GIRL—MY MATEA—WHERE IS SHE?" GROOT CARLUS ASKED EAGERLY. THE STRANGER SHRUGGED.

"I DON'T KNOW, BUT I'M TAKING YOU TO A FELLOW WHO TOLD ME HE SAW HER BROUGHT HERE."

PRESENTLY THE MAN USHERED THEM INTO A HALL WITH A NARROW STAIRWAY. "GO ON UP!" HE INVITED.

UNITED FEATURE SYNDICATE, Inc.

TARZAN HESITATED. LIKE ALL JUNGLE CREATURES HE WAS SUSPICIOUS OF UNFAMILIAR ENCLOSURES.

BUT GROOT CARLUS, IMPATIENT TO FIND A CLUE TO MATEA, URGED HIM ON.

THEY WERE SHOWN INTO A ROOM WHERE SAT A BEARDED MAN. TO TARZAN HE WAS HAUNTINGLY FAMILIAR —YET UNFAMILIAR.

"I KNOW WHERE THE GIRL IS," SAID THE BEARDED MAN, "BUT IT'LL TAKE SOME FIGHTING TO GET HER."

MEANWHILE, TRIGGER BOYLE SOUGHT OUT TWO MEN AND WHISPERED TO THEM EXCITEDLY. "TARZAN AND THE BIG GUY ARE AT THE BOSS'S PLACE. WE'RE GOING TO DO THE JOB NOW. LET'S GO!"

HOGARTH—

NEXT WEEK: THE VILLAIN UNMASKED

STAR OF AFRICA HOTEL

Tarzan

by EDGAR RICE BURROUGHS

470-3-10-40

THE VILLAIN UNMASKED

TRIGGER BOYLE AND HIS COMPANIONS HURRIED STEALTHILY TOWARD THE ROOM WHERE----

--TARZAN AND GROOT CARLUS TALKED WITH THE BEARDED STRANGER ABOUT MATEA'S RESCUE.

CARLUS WAS IMPATIENT FOR ACTION, BUT THE MAN STALLED: "IT'S DANGEROUS. WE MUST PREPARE A PLAN."

MEANWHILE, BO-DAN HAD FOLLOWED TARZAN, AND NOW HE BARKED AND SCRATCHED AT THE DOOR.

"MY PET BABOON," TARZAN SMILED. THE STRANGER WENT PALE ABOVE HIS BEARD. "SEND HIM AWAY. I HATE BABOONS."

AS TARZAN OPENED THE DOOR, BO-DAN'S NOSE QUIVERED. THERE WAS A FAMILIAR SCENT HERE--A HATED SCENT.

OBEYING TARZAN, THE BABOON WENT OUTSIDE TO WAIT, BUT THAT SCENT HAUNTED AND INFLAMED HIM.

HE CLIMBED TO THE WINDOW OF THE ROOM AND PEERED OVER THE SILL AT THE BEARDED MAN.

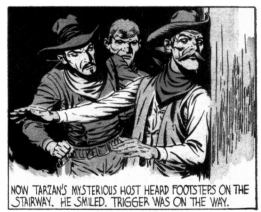

NOW TARZAN'S MYSTERIOUS HOST HEARD FOOTSTEPS ON THE STAIRWAY. HE SMILED. TRIGGER WAS ON THE WAY.

THEN SUDDENLY BO-DAN HURLED HIMSELF AT THE STRANGER. "HELP! TAKE HIM AWAY!" THE MAN SCREAMED.

HOGARTH—

"KLAAS VANGER!" GROOT CARLUS EXCLAIMED. AT THAT MOMENT THE DOOR FLEW OPEN!

IN HIS PANIC HE FORGOT TO DISGUISE HIS VOICE. AND BO-DAN'S TUG AT HIS BEARD REVEALED THE TELLTALE SCAR.

NEXT WEEK: SHOWDOWN

Tarzan
by EDGAR RICE BURROUGHS
SHOWDOWN

471-3-17-40

FIRST TO PENETRATE THE VILLAIN'S DISGUISE, BO-DAN LEAPED AT KLAAS VANGER.

AS THE MAN SCREAMED, GROOT CARLUS RECOGNIZED HIM AND STRODE TOWARD HIM.

THEN THE DOOR FLEW OPEN. VANGER'S HENCHMEN BURST IN.

ONE FIRED. GROOT CARLUS STAGGERED BACK, BUT KEPT HIS FEET.

WITH THE GUNMEN COVERING HIS RETREAT, THE COWARDLY VANGER SHOOK OFF BO-DAN AND RAN FOR THE DOOR.

Copr. 1940, Edgar Rice Burroughs, Inc.—Tm. Reg. U.S. Pat. Off. Produced in Famous Books and Plays. Distributed by UNITED FEATURE SYNDICATE, Inc.

"FINISH 'EM OFF," HE CALLED BACK AS HE FLED.

NOW TARZAN WHIPPED AN ARROW FROM HIS QUIVER AND FLUNG IT AS A DART.

ONE OF THE GUNMEN FELL, BUT ANOTHER POINTED HIS REVOLVER AT TARZAN.

THE WOUNDED CARLUS FLOORED HIM WITH A POWERFUL BLOW.

THEN TRIGGER BOYLE TOOK CAREFUL AIM AT TARZAN.

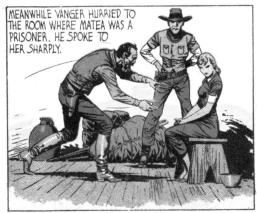

MEANWHILE VANGER HURRIED TO THE ROOM WHERE MATEA WAS A PRISONER. HE SPOKE TO HER SHARPLY.

"WE'RE MOVING--QUICK! I'M TAKING NO CHANCES ON HAVING YOU GRABBED AWAY FROM ME!"

NEXT WEEK: **PLAN FOR AMBUSH**

HOGARTH

Tarzan

by Edgar Rice Burroughs

3-24-40

PLAN FOR AMBUSH

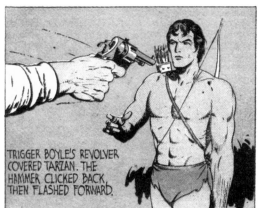

TRIGGER BOYLE'S REVOLVER COVERED TARZAN. THE HAMMER CLICKED BACK, THEN FLASHED FORWARD.

AT THAT INSTANT, BO-DAN LEAPED AT THE MAN'S ARM. THE BULLET WENT WILD.

A MOMENT LATER THE APE-MAN FELLED BOYLE WITH A POWERFUL BLOW.

WHEN THEIR ENEMIES WERE DISPOSED OF, GROOT CARLUS CRIED, "NOW TO SAVE MY MATEA, MY BELOVED MATEA."

MEANWHILE, VANGER WAS HASTILY PREPARING TO FLEE WITH THE UNFORTUNATE GIRL.

FROM A WINDOW TARZAN SAW THE VILLAIN RIDING AWAY WITH HIS VICTIM. DOWN TO THE STREET HE LEAPED.

HE RAN TO GRASP THE HORSE'S BRIDLE. VANGER JERKED THE REINS. THE HORSE REARED AND STRUCK TARZAN DOWN.

AS VANGER GALLOPED AWAY, THE APE-MAN ROSE AND MOUNTED HIS OWN HORSE. BO-DAN LEAPED UP BEHIND HIM.

ACROSS THE VELDT HE GAVE CHASE, WITH GROOT CARLUS BESIDE HIM. AHEAD THE FUGITIVES OPENED FIRE.

TARZAN AND CARLUS, RIDING VALIANTLY, GRADUALLY GAINED ON THEIR QUARRY.

HERE HE'D FIND SAFE AMBUSH FROM WHICH TO SLAY HIS PURSUERS! NEXT WEEK: **VILLAIN'S SHIELD**

AT LAST VANGER TURNED INTO DUIVELSKLOOF, THE MYSTERIOUS RAVINE.

HOGARTH—

Tarzan

by EDGAR RICE BURROUGHS

VILLAIN'S SHIELD

WITH MATEA CAPTIVE, VANGER AND HIS HENCHMAN TURNED INTO DUIVELSKLOOF, TO AMBUSH THEIR PURSUERS.

AT THE MOUTH OF THE RAVINE, TARZAN HALTED AND GAVE INSTRUCTIONS TO BO-DAN AND CARLUS.

THE APE-MAN HIMSELF DISMOUNTED AND DISAPPEARED AMONG THE BOULDERS.

NOW AND THEN HE PAUSED AND LIFTED HIS VOICE IN A SHRILL BEAST CRY.

HIGH IN THE CANYON THE BABOONS HEARD HIM. "OUR FRIEND TARZAN CALLS," THEY SAID; "WE GO!"

MEANWHILE, AS TARZAN ORDERED, GROOT CARLUS DASHED AFTER THE CRIMINALS.

WHEN HE CAME IN SIGHT, VANGER OPENED FIRE. CARLUS DARED NOT ANSWER FOR FEAR OF HARMING MATEA.

THEN, SUDDENLY, VANGER'S FLIGHT WAS HALTED BY A GIANT CLIFF RISING FROM THE FLOOR OF THE RAVINE

WITH A SNARL HE TURNED HIS REVOLVER AGAIN ON HIS PURSUER NOW THAT HE WAS STILL, HIS AIM WAS BETTER.

CARLUS LEAPED FROM HIS HORSE AND CREPT FORWARD THROUGH THE BUSHES, SEEKING A CLEAR SHOT AT HIS QUARRY

BUT VANGER JERKED MATEA IN FRONT OF HIM AND THRUST HIS REVOLVER AT HER HEAD.

"MAKE ANOTHER MOVE," HE SHOUTED TO CARLUS, "AND I'LL FIRE!"

NEXT WEEK: MISFORTUNE

HOGARTH—

Tarzan
by Edgar Rice Burroughs

MISFORTUNE

AS VANGER PRESSED THE REVOLVER AGAINST MATEA, HE CALLED TO GROOT CARLUS:"STAY WHERE YOU ARE- OR SHE DIES!"

"COWARD!" CARLUS ROARED. "A WOMAN FOR A SHIELD! COME OUT! WITH ONE HAND I FIGHT YOU!"

MEANWHILE, BO-DAN WAS HURRYING TO ROUND UP THE BABOONS. HE FOUND THEM RALLYING TO TARZAN'S CALL.

WHEN THEY WERE GATHERED, TARZAN SPOKE:"THE EVIL TARMANGANI HAS RETURNED. THIS TIME HE MUST DIE!"

"HE MUST DIE!" NODDED A DOUGHTY WARRIOR. AND THE OTHERS ECHOED OMINOUSLY, "MUST DIE!"

SO THE JUNGLE LORD LED HIS STRANGE TROOP TO THE GREAT BARRIER WHERE HE KNEW VANGER WOULD BE HALTED.

FAR BELOW HE HEARD THE VILLAINS COMMANDING CARLUS: "THROW DOWN YOUR GUN AND LET US PASS!"

TARZAN KNEW HE MUST ACT QUICKLY IF THE SCOUNDREL WAS TO BE TRAPPED. BECKONING HIS HAIRY COHORTS---

----HE STARTED DOWN THE SHEER FACE OF THE CLIFF.

THEN--- CALAMITY! A BABOON STEPPED ON A LOOSE ROCK. A CASCADE OF STONES THUNDERED DOWN!

VANGER WHIRLED AND GLANCED UP. THERE WAS TARZAN CLINGING TO THE WALL ABOVE, A PERFECT TARGET!

HOGARTH

474-4-7-40

THE VILLAIN CALLED TO HIS HENCHMAN. "PICK OFF THE BABOONS. TARZAN IS MINE!"

NEXT WEEK: **FAIR IS FOUL!**

Tarzan
by Edgar Rice Burroughs

FAIR
IS FOUL

VANGER TOOK AIM AT TARZAN, AND FIRED! AT THE SAME INSTANT A LIGHTNING CHAIN OF ACTION WAS LET LOOSE.

BRAVE MATEA STRUCK UP THE VILLAIN'S ARM. TARZAN LEAPED ON VANGER. THE BABOONS SAILED DOWN INTO THE FRAY.

GROOT CARLUS DASHED UP, ROARING: "VANGER IS MINE!" SO TARZAN DROVE THE BABOONS AWAY AND JERKED THE VILLAIN TO HIS FEET.

CARLUS SPOKE SOLEMNLY: "YOU WILL HAVE A CHANCE TO FIGHT LIKE A MAN!"

"BUT YOU ARE BIGGER," VANGER WHINED. CARLUS NODDED, THEN STRODE TO ONE OF THE HORSES AND CUT A REIN.

TO TARZAN HE HANDED THE LEATHER THONG, AND SAID: "YOU WILL BIND MY RIGHT ARM TO MY SIDE!"

Copr. 1940, Edgar Rice Burroughs, Inc.—Tm Reg U S Pat.
Off. Produced by Famous Books and Plays. Distributed by
UNITED FEATURE SYNDICATE, Inc.

THEN HE TURNED TO HIS FOE. "WITH MY LEFT ARM ALONE I FIGHT YOU, KLAAS VANGER——TO THE DEATH!" "NO-NO!" MATEA PLEADED: "HE DESERVES NO SUCH OPPORTUNITY. OH, BRAVE, FOOLISH CARLUS, I LOVE YOU. AND HE MAY KILL YOU!"

"AYE, SO HE MAY," THE GIANT AGREED, "BUT NO ONE CAN SAY THAT GROOT CARLUS WAS NOT A JUST MAN, EVEN TO HIS ENEMIES!"

TARZAN DID AS HE WAS BIDDEN, WITHOUT PROTEST. HE KNEW HIS FRIEND'S FANATIC, HEROIC DEVOTION TO FAIR PLAY.

"ON GUARD!" CALLED CARLUS TO VANGER. THEN TO TARZAN. "NO MATTER WHAT HAPPENS, YOU WILL NOT INTERFERE———PROMISE!"

TARZAN NODDED CONSENT. THREE MINUTES LATER HE WAS SORRY!
NEXT WEEK:
TREACHERY

HOGARTH—

475-4-14-40

Tarzan and the Boers, Part II   165

Tarzan

by EDGAR RICE BURROUGHS

TREACHERY

WITH HIS RIGHT ARM STRAPPED, CARLUS ADVANCED. "NOW WE'RE EQUAL," HE CALLED. "WE FIGHT WITH OUR HANDS—TO THE DEATH!"

IN A LOW CROUCH, VANGER CIRCLED THE BIG FELLOW, AS IF SEARCHING FOR AN OPENING.

"OH, MYNHEER TARZAN," MATEA PLEADED TEARFULLY, "YOU MUST HELP CARLUS. VANGER HAS THE ADVANTAGE."

THE APE-MAN SHOOK HIS HEAD. "CARLUS MADE ME PROMISE NOT TO INTERFERE."

MATEA RECOGNIZED ONLY ONE FACT. THE MAN SHE LOVED WAS IN PERIL. WITH THE FURY OF A LIONESS SHE DASHED AT VANGER. "OUT OF THE WAY, MATEA. YOU'LL BE HURT!" THE GIANT CRIED. BUT THE GIRL DID NOT HEED.

THE VILLAIN SEIZED HER AND FLUNG HER VIOLENTLY TO THE GROUND.

GROOT CARLUS, USUALLY UNEXCITABLE, EMITTED A BELLOW OF RAGE, AND CHARGED RECKLESSLY.

VANGER RAN TOWARD ONE OF THE HORSES, READY TO ESCAPE WHEN HE HAD STRUCK HIS TREACHEROUS BLOW.

SUDDENLY HE HALTED. HIS RIGHT HAND DIPPED INSIDE HIS SHIRT. OUT CAME A KNIFE.

CARLUS TRIED TO CHECK HIS HEADLONG RUSH; TO DODGE. THE AWKWARD GIANT SLIPPED ON A ROCK AND FELL. WITH A CRY OF TRIUMPH, THE SCOUNDREL POUNCED UPON HIM! NEXT WEEK: *JUSTICE IS DONE*

Tarzan

by EDGAR RICE BURROUGHS

JUSTICE IS DONE

AS GROOT CARLUS SLIPPED AND FELL BACKWARD, VANGER CHARGED HIM.

WHEN THE TREACHEROUS SCOUNDREL DREW A KNIFE, TARZAN CONSIDERED HIMSELF RELEASED FROM HIS PROMISE NOT TO INTERFERE.

HE DASHED FORWARD TO AID HIS LUCKLESS FRIEND. BUT CARLUS NEEDED NO AID.

HE DREW BACK A FOOT AND DROVE IT INTO VANGER'S MIDRIFF. THE VILLAIN FLEW BACKWARD.

CARLUS LEAPED UP AND GRAPPLED WITH HIS FOE. IN THE STRUGGLE THE KNIFE PIERCED VANGER'S HEART. JUSTICE WAS DONE!

MEANWHILE, THE BABOONS ACCOUNTED FOR VANGER'S ACCOMPLICE.

BO-DAN STRUTTED, PROUD OF HIS PART IN THE DAY'S EXCITEMENT. "I AM THE MIGHTY TARZAN OF THE BABOONS," HE BOASTED.

HUGE CARLUS PUT AN ARM AWKWARDLY AROUND MATEA, AND THEY STARTED HOMEWARD.

ON THE WAY, TARZAN DISCOVERED THE DIAMOND DEPOSIT VANGER HAD FOUND. HE STEERED CARLUS AND MATEA AROUND IT.

THEY'D BE HAPPIER, HE KNEW, IN THE SIMPLE LIFE OF THE GREAT VELDT, UNTOUCHED BY THE TRAPPINGS OF RICHES.

WHEN TARZAN BADE FAREWELL TO THE VAN BOERENS CARLUS SAID SIMPLY, "IF YOU EVER NEED ME, I WILL COME!"

A WEEK LATER, TARZAN NEEDED SUCH AN ALLY AS CARLUS MORE THAN EVER BEFORE IN HIS ADVENTUROUS LIFE! 477-4-28-40
NEXT WEEK: **A COWARD'S TRICK!**